REFORM THE
KAKISTOCRACY

Rule by the Least Able or Least Principled Citizens

William L. Kovacs

NEWMAN SPRINGS PUBLISHING
320 Broad Street
Red Bank, NJ 07701

First originally published by Newman Springs Publishing 2019

ISBN 978-1-64096-514-0 (Paperback)
ISBN 978-1-64096-515-7 (Digital)

Printed in the United States of America

This book is dedicated to the Dutiful Cog, that person who keeps society running by getting up every day and going to work, taking care of family, paying taxes, contributing to community, and being continuously loyal to the nation. The Dutiful Cog asks for little other than simple fairness and to be left invisible, while enduring the many petty insults thrown upon him or her by the kakistocracy. While the Dutiful Cog may feel powerless while holding our society together, he or she fails to appreciate that, as a group, Cogs are the only people in society who can radically change it. All the Dutiful Cogs need do is vote in large numbers and change will occur because those running the kakistocracy will turn on each other, believing that they can preserve their status and privilege by sacrificing others. In the end, there is no honor within the kakistocracy; that is why the Dutiful Cogs will prevail.

Contents

What Is Kakistocracy? 9

What Hath the Kakistocracy Wrought? 11

Who Runs the Kakistocracy? 19

Part I: How It Is

How It Is..37

The Kakistocrats Have Forgotten Their Oaths 38

The Kakistocrats Have Rewritten the US Constitution 41

The Kakistocrats Are Imposing Involuntary Servitude on
    Us and Our Posterity...44

Complex Governments Are Corrupt 48

The Kakistocrats Are Regulating Our Nation Out of
    Business and the New Sheriff Can't Stop It!..........................51

The Kakistocracy Is a Political Soundstage Managed by
    Scarecrows..55

Beware of the Kakistocrats' Dodgery and Jobbery.......................59

The Kakistocrats Are the Ultimate Special Interest 63

Our Republic Will Not End by Invasion but by the
    Gavel and by Preachers of Hate and Resentment.................66

Part II: Principles of Federal Governance

Need for a Federal Governance Policy 71

Governance Principle 1: Kakistocrats Do Not Have
    Rights, Only Responsibilities...73

Governance Principle 2: Kakistocrats Must Become Fiduciaries...75

Governance Principle 3: The Privileges of the
Kakistocracy Must Be Abolished 77

Governance Principle 4: There Must Be Real Checks
and Balances Between Branches of Government..................79

Governance Principle 5: The Executive and the Courts
Must Voluntarily Limit Their Legislating Activities
to Preserve the Constitution 81

Governance Principle 6: Laws Must Be Reduced and Simplified .84

Governance Principle 7: The Functions of Government
Must Be Performed at the Most Efficient Level of
Government 86

Governance Principle 8: Government Must Focus on Priorities...88

Governance Principle 9: Government Must Be More
Than Transparent—It Must Be Understandable 90

Governance Principle 10: Government Must Operate
Only for the Public Purpose 92

Part III: A Few Modest Proposals for Restructuring the Kakistocracy

The Kakistocracy's Breach of Its Fiduciary Duty
Necessitates Its Restructuring 97

Restructuring Proposal 1: Congress Must Reclaim Its
Role as the Primary Legislative Body 100

Restructuring Proposal 2: Restructuring of the
Kakistocracy Must Include Everything the
Kakistocrats Manage 102

Restructuring Proposal 3: The Kakistocracy Must
Devolve Power to the States...104

Restructuring Proposal 4: Congress Must Reestablish the
Joint Committee on the Reduction of Nonessential
Federal Expenditures 107

Restructuring Proposal 5: Spending Must Be Limited to
    Essential Activities 109

Restructuring Proposal 6: Congress Must Not
    Appropriate Money for Unauthorized Laws 111

Restructuring Proposal 7: Regulatory Complexity Must
    Be Reversed 115

Restructuring Proposal 8: The Kakistocracy Must Sell
    All Unnecessary Assets 119

Restructuring Proposal 9: The Western Lands Must Be
    Returned to the States 121

Restructuring Proposal 10: Congress Should Not Give
    Taxpayer Money to Private Entities 123

Restructuring Proposal 11: It Must Not Be Financially
    Attractive to Stay in the Kakistocracy 126

Restructuring Proposal 12: States Need to Assume Their
    Constitutional Role in Governing the Nation 128

Part IV: Restructuring the Automatic Withdrawals of Taxpayer Assets

How Well We Treat Our People Will Determine How
    Long Our Constitutional Republic Lasts 133

The Kakistocracy Can Easily Fix Social Security 137

Fixing Health Care Will Require the Wisdom of Our Founders . 141

Taxes: Eliminate Complexity, Unfairness, and Tax-
    Avoidance Schemes 149

Part V: Citizen Management of the Kakistocracy

It Is Now! 161

Principles for Citizen Management of the Kakistocracy 163

Citizens Must Demand That Elected Kakistocrats Take
    the Gift Clause Pledge 166

Establish a Citizen Information Center 168

Citizens Can Start a Glorious Constitutional Revolution 170

States Can Start a Glorious Constitutional Revolution 173

What Would Devolution of Federal Government Powers
    to the States Look Like?..176

Going Forward

We Have Reached a Fork in the Road 181

What Is Kakistocracy?

Kakistocracy, rule by the least able or least principled citizens, is a form of government in which the people least qualified to control the government are the people who control the government.

The origin of this word is Greek, derived from the superlative of the adjective "*kakos*" (bad), "*kakistos*" (worst).

What Hath the Kakistocracy Wrought?

The Dutiful Cog asks a simple question: What hath the kakistocracy wrought?

It put us more than twenty-one trillion dollars in debt by borrowing money that future generations will have to repay.

It exposed the nation to countless trillions of dollars of potential liability by making promises it cannot keep.

Its federal civil servants, people we handsomely compensate with salary and pensions, owe more than $1 billion in back taxes.

It confirmed nominees to high office who failed to pay their income taxes.

It created an entitlement system that, if not changed, will impose more than $45 trillion of costs on future generations.

It gave us a health-care system that costs twice as much as that of any other industrialized nation, yet our nation has a life expectancy four years shorter than other major countries.

It gave us "Fast and Furious," which has resulted in Mexican drug dealers capturing our guns and then using them to kill our people.

It gave us Benghazi, where our ambassador and other embassy staff were killed, and our government did not even come to their rescue or attempt to defend them.

It gave us a tax-collection agency, the Internal Revenue Service, which investigates organizations that disagree with the president's political views by denying the organizations the right to have their applications reviewed like any other American.

It gave us the National Security Administration, which spies on the American people.

It turned our Social Security system into a real Ponzi scheme by using our excess payments to fund current government programs and then requiring future generations of Americans to pay for the promises made to current retirees.

It developed policies that collapsed the real-estate market by fostering the purchase of homes by people with few assets and insufficient income to cover their mortgage and then allowed the industry to repackage the assets and fraudulently sell them to investors as being of the highest quality.

It enacted laws that allowed our banking system to turn into a casino, using the deposits of hardworking people for risky investments that, if successful, would greatly benefit the banks and, if unsuccessful, required the American people to absorb the loss, thereby causing the collapse of the banking system in 2008, the worst financial crisis since the Great Depression.

It allowed the bailed-out banks to use our money to bestow multimillion-dollar bonuses on the bankers who caused the massive financial crisis in 2008.

It allowed the creation of transactions, such as credit default swaps, that are so complex, only computers can manage them; such transactions were not understood by those selling them to investors, thus causing massive financial losses.

It fostered the delegation of vast legislative powers from Congress to unelected regulators.

It tolerated the appropriation of hundreds of billions of dollars to pay for programs that had not been reauthorized by Congress for decades.

It appropriated money and awarded it to political friends to build housing for the poor that was never built.

It gave tens of billions of dollars of subsidies, for decades, to energy projects that were never economically viable and could produce only small amounts of energy.

It paid members of Congress salaries greater than those of ninety percent of all income earners in the nation.

It tolerated members of Congress giving themselves automatic pay increases, no matter how poorly they performed, no matter how little they accomplished.

It granted large subsidies to the wealthiest agricultural corporations at a time when commodity prices were at all-time highs.

It used our tax dollars to subsidize the purchase of flood insurance by the wealthiest Americans so they could build and rebuild beach houses—near water subject to flooding—at our expense.

It negligently designed and built levees around New Orleans that collapsed, resulting in devastation to the city and its people during Hurricane Katrina.

It demonstrated incompetence in the management of the Katrina disaster, such as by supplying temporary homes containing mold and toxic substances.

It appropriated such vast amounts of federal money to address natural disasters where our money could not effectively be spent, and much of it was wasted or used for purposes other than addressing the disaster.

It drove up the cost of higher education by making loans freely available to students, thus allowing colleges to increase tuition far in excess of the rate of inflation and the value of the service provided.

It accelerated income inequality through poor tax policy and a failure to create economic opportunity.

It drove down the real incomes of the American people to levels that existed decades ago.

It increased the federal bureaucracy by increasing the layers of bureaucracy from seven to eighteen and swelling the number of bureaucrats per layer from four hundred and fifty-one to two thousand and six hundred in only a few decades.

It allowed federal agencies to host lavish parties at taxpayer expense.

It exempted Congress from insider stock-trading rules, whereas breaking those rules would be considered criminal if done by a private citizen.

It established dual compliance standards, allowing agencies like the Securities and Exchange Commission to demand corporate compliance with all accounting rules but allowing federal agencies to have millions of dollars of accounting errors on their books and tolerating accounting schemes that intentionally mislead the American people, which would be criminal offenses if done by a private-sector company.

It failed to provide our war veterans with mental and physical injuries the adequate care they need.

It demonstrated gross incompetence in managing the Veterans Administration hospital system.

It played games in budget deals with the death benefits that are given to our brave soldiers, just to shame political opponents.

It permitted our war veterans to be maltreated and forced to live in filthy conditions at Walter Reed Army Medical Center while permitting the hospital to establish a caste system as a means of allocating services.

It hid from workers at nuclear weapons facilities the fact that cleaning up spills inside nuclear facilities causes cancer and then denied them compensation for their cancer.

It encouraged the skyrocketing use of noncompete federal contracts, which greatly increased the costs of the projects for taxpayers.

It increased the number of government contractors to 7.5 million, which is a hidden workforce, but fostered the impression that the federal government workforce remained at a reasonable size.

It allowed spouses, children, and relatives of members of Congress to receive and prosper nicely from federal contracts.

It assisted congressional family members in securing high-paying jobs in lobbying, real estate, public relations, and other activities where the organization hiring the family member could benefit directly from the hire.

It tolerated members of Congress evading taxes.

It placed the cost of many wars off the books by paying for them through a supplemental appropriation that is not counted as part of the budget deficit.

It tolerated, for decades, a revolving door that allows thousands of government employees to use their contacts in government to secure high-paying jobs in the private sector and then return to government to refresh their contacts and gain additional inside information so they can return to the private sector for even higher salaries.

It tolerated members of Congress purchasing land from friends at vastly discounted prices and using inside information for development of the land.

It allowed infrastructure projects to be built near land owned by members of Congress so as to significantly increase the value of the land and the members' wealth.

It awarded grants and contracts to political allies, even those without the expertise to complete the jobs.

It used personal information in government databases against political opponents.

It accepted the inability of the IRS to catch tax cheats, which costs the American people hundreds of billions of dollars annually while raising our taxes and the taxes of future generations.

It is incapable of passing a budget for the nation year after year.

It tolerates a federal Railroad Retirement Board that approves ninety-eight percent of all disability claims, thereby putting the entire railroad retirement system at risk when compensating real disabilities.

It releases terrorists from prison, thereby allowing them to again commit acts of terrorism.

It viewed the Islamic State as a junior varsity team at a time when it was a well-managed killing machine.

It allowed a secretary of state to place the security of the nation at risk through the improper handling of unsecured e-mails.

It allowed a former president, while his wife was secretary of state, to raise hundreds of millions of dollars for his family foundation while he was making tens of millions of dollars in speeches and consulting.

It has a political party rigging primary elections, a clear destruction of democracy and the right to vote.

Many members of Congress and executive-branch officers serve in public office mostly to cash in on public service by later lobbying friendly government officials, writing "tell-all" books, and aggressively using connections in government.

Congress continuously drafts its most important legislation in secret, with selected members of Congress and collaborators, but without public participation.

Several members of Congress put nude photographs of themselves on the internet.

Several members of Congress were buying drugs on the floor of the House of Representatives and using them in their private bathrooms and were not prosecuted.

Congress and the executive branch maintain secret funds so that legal claims against them can be settled in secret.

High-ranking officials violate laws protecting national security and remain free, while members of our armed forces take unauthorized photographs and are sentenced to prison.

The Federal Bureau of Investigation and the Department of Justice refuse to provide requested materials to Congress so that it can conduct oversight of the agencies, and Congress is powerless to force compliance.

Federal investigations in which the key documents relating to the alleged crimes of prominent government officials are "lost" by the government.

Federal officers use fake names for e-mail addresses to avoid having to comply with the Freedom of Information Act and disclosure of their actions as officers in our government.

The Department of Justice and the Federal Bureau of Investigation are found to have a culture of leaking classified documents to the press in return for tickets to non-public social events, golf outings, dinners, drinks and other gifts.

It was also found that even the federal investigators investigating the President had bias.

The Director of the Federal Bureau of Investigation is found to be insubordinate by unlawfully assuming the powers of the Attorney General of the United States by interfering with a presidential election.

Members of our government degrade themselves and civil society by publicly insulting each other and by calling on citizens to harass other members of our government. The continuation of such conduct increases the potential for violence in our society.

The entire political system has become one of unverified accusations leveled to destroy political opponents rather than to operate the government to help build a better life for its citizens.

***

After decades of the government embracing and fostering the conduct described above, there is only one term in the language of man that can adequately describe what it has become. Our government is now a kakistocracy, rule by the least able or least principled citizens. These "leaders" we shall call kakistocrats.

How does one even respond to the kakistocracy? Though they would like to be treated as royalty, which they believe they are, the more proper response may be one based on the speech given by Oliver Cromwell, in England's House of Commons, at 11:00 a.m. on April 20, 1653, to the Rump Parliament on its dissolution:

> It is high time for me to put an end to your sitting in this place, which you have dishonored by your contempt of all virtue, and defiled by your practice of every vice; ye are a factious crew, and enemies to all good government; ye are a pack of mercenary wretches, and would like Esau sell your country for a mess of pottage, and like Judas betray your God for a few pieces of money.
>
> Is there a single virtue now remaining amongst you? Is there one vice you do not possess? Ye have no more religion than my horse; gold is your God; which of you have not barter'd your conscience for bribes? Is there a man amongst you that has the least care for the good of the Commonwealth?
>
> Ye sordid prostitutes have you not defil'd this sacred place, and turn'd the Lord's temple into a den of thieves, by your immoral principles and wicked practices? Ye are grown intolerably

odious to the whole nation; you were deputed here by the people to get grievances redress'd, are yourselves gone! So! Take away that shining bauble there, and lock up the doors.

In the name of God, go!

Who Runs the Kakistocracy?

The kakistocracy is run by two groups: the kakistocrats and the collabortakers.

Kakistocrats are members of Congress, judges, the president, and the bureaucrats who occupy the thousands of positions in our government, whom we pay handsomely for the management of our country. These are the people who make, enforce, interpret and reinterpret hundreds of thousands of laws and regulations that govern almost every aspect of our lives. These are the people who determine if we are free or imprisoned, safe or at risk, rich or poor.

Collabortakers are a group of people working together to take something. In a kakistocracy, the group collaborates with the kakistocrats to create a legal system that allows them to take as much of the wealth of the nation as they can take without inciting a revolt by the Dutiful Cogs.

The word "collabortakers" is a linguistic blend of two words, "collaborator" and "taker," to form a new word that more accurately captures the actions of these individuals and organizations that collaborate with the kakistocracy so they may have access to the wealth of the nation. The collabortakers include lobbyists, friends of the kakistocrats, corporations, political action committees, unions, social-engineering activists, trade associations, think tanks, communicators, and political parties.

Let's meet the kakistocrats.

1. *Congress*, the one institution that could do so much but does so little. We elect and pay its presumably well-intentioned, public-spirited, underachieving members to repre-

sent us and only us in making the laws that we live under. In short, it is truly our board of directors, the group that takes an oath to be bound by and support the Constitution of the United States. [The terms Constitution of the United States, US Constitution or Constitution are used interchangeably throughout.] As such, members of Congress should not act in the interest of any specific individual, group, or political entity but as a fiduciary for the nation, that is, to act in the best interests of the nation without regard for personal gain.

The concept of the members of a legislature being fiduciaries originates with John Locke in his *Two Treatises of Government*, in which he argues that government and governed cannot operate by contract because, under a contract, both parties receive benefit. Locke believed that the government and those acting on behalf of the government cannot benefit from their positions. Therefore, governing is a relationship of trust, and those governing are in a fiduciary relationship with the citizens who are the beneficiaries of the relationship.

Unfortunately, members of Congress very much enjoy being in Congress, with the salary, lifetime pension, and many other perks that are substantially better than what almost all the citizens they represent receive. They have titles that most average American citizens deride but that those in Washington, DC, show great respect for, because each member of Congress has some access to our money. Collabortakers make sure that members of Congress get the best deals on anything they need, including partnerships, new cars, real estate, jobs for family members, or scholarships for their kids. The job is so great that from the moment they are elected, the goal of most members of Congress is to keep their job. And they believe that the best way to keep it is to help the collabortakers help them stay in office.

They avoid the major issues facing the nation, because they involve difficult decisions that have real consequences. As making difficult decisions will always anger some citizens, kakistocrats believe the best decision is to run away and fight another day, which they hope will never arrive but always does. For these reasons, Congress allows the nation to drift by avoiding the exercise of its most fundamental constitutional powers: declaring war, preparing and agreeing upon budgets for the nation, appropriating funds to run the nation, managing the debts of the nation, and overseeing the operation of the nation to "promote the general Welfare and secure the Blessings of Liberty to ourselves and our Posterity." With the avoidance of decision-making and the fact that, for the last half-century, Congress has delegated massive amounts of its legislative authority to the federal bureaucracy by passing broad, vague laws, the American citizen now lives with a government under which real laws are made by unelected bureaucrats, and Congress does not possess the understanding, vision, or courage to take back legislative control of our government.

In short, to these "giants on Capitol Hill," our Constitution has become a quaint, antiquated document with little relevance to their responsibilities. Congress takes the first seat at the table, since it is the only institution in our government that can actually control the nation's purse while acting as a check on the excessive policy-making activities of the executive, the bureaucracy, and the courts. But to assume such control over the legislative process, it must act as the institution of Congress performing its Article I legislative functions, not as the handmaiden of the executive branch, political parties, and the collabortakers.

2. *The president* is our chief executive officer. As such, this is the only person in the nation we elect to take care that the laws passed by Congress are faithfully executed and to command our armed forces. To exercise these powers, the

21

president is authorized to appoint executive-branch officials, nominate judges, recommend measures to Congress as judged necessary and veto legislation subject to congressional override. From such clear, direct, and limited constitutional powers has grown an office so large and powerful that the wrong occupant, through the management of the bureaucracy, could assume control over all aspects of human activity in the United States, and citizens would be powerless to respond. And at some future time, there will be a president who will do just that, unless Congress and the courts are capable of checking the president's exercise of power using the administrative state.

The president controls the nation, since Congress delegated to the executive branch vast legislative authority and the money to use it by controlling millions of bureaucrats who, on a daily basis, issue countless and largely unread regulations that determine what the laws mean when passed by Congress. The President also assumes the war-making power of Congress by regularly waging war without a congressional declaration of war.

3. *The courts* are the only institution in our federal government that have no elected officers and whose officers, judges, are appointed for life and free to rule in any manner, subject only to occasional review by a higher court. The purpose of having an independent judiciary is to have independent citizens protect individuals from the abuses of the legislature or the executive.

While an independent judiciary is essential to a constitutional government of limited powers, the judiciary has become just another political branch of government. Individuals are appointed or denied appointment to a court based on political belief, political affiliation, and the support of kakistocrats. Occasionally, these judges will stray from the beliefs of the political party supporting their elevation to the federal courts, but for the most part, their decisions reliably carry out what is expected of them by their kakistocrat supporters. Such reliability transforms an independent judiciary that is to operate as a real check on the excesses of the other branches of government into a political weapon against the Constitution. Recent illustrations of the courts implementing political beliefs rather than sound legal reasoning are found in lower-court judges with jurisdiction limited to the district in which they serve and to the disputes of the parties before the court. In 2017 alone, several judges sitting on courts of limited jurisdiction, for political reasons, issued nationwide injunctions that directly intrude on the power of the executive branch and the laws passed by Congress.

The combination of congressionally enacted laws that are broad and vague and require a bureaucracy to determine their meaning and judicial deference that supports the meaning of the law applied by the bureaucracy ensures that we the people will live without the real checks and balances our founders intended us to have. In the final analysis, the courts have generally become active participants in the transformation of the Constitution into a purely political document that changes with the political winds—and certainly the political beliefs of judges.

4. *The bureaucrat* is the heartbeat of the administrative state. It is the faceless person who writes, interprets, and enforces the rules or regulations (these terms are used interchangeably throughout) that manage our country. There are millions of bureaucrats who have carefully crafted hundreds of thousands of incomprehensible regulations totaling more words and pages than any human would ever read. Yet it is the bureaucrat who interprets what the laws of Congress mean and how we need to obey those laws. It is also the bureaucrat who enforces the laws against us.

The bureaucrat is looked upon by the courts as an expert in deciphering how to implement the laws passed by Congress. Because of this so-called expertise, the courts put their common sense and fact-finding skills aside and give great deference to the opinion of the bureaucrat. Growing up, we are taught that all individuals are presumed to know the law. Unfortunately, in reality, not one person can possibly know all the law, which now comprises hundreds of thousands of statutes, regulations interpreting the statutes, and guidance interpreting the regulations, along with bureaucrats interpreting and enforcing the statutes, regulations, and guidance according to their own discretion.

These bureaucrats do not know us, and neither do we usually know them. We have contact with them when they confront us for doing something they believe to be wrong or impose requirements on us that many times we cannot comprehend. Most of us break the bureaucrats' laws every day, but we avoid punishment, mainly because there are not enough bureaucrats to enforce all their regulations. But if the bureaucrat wants to "get" you or me, there is always a law or regulation that justifies his or her actions.

In the end, we generally know these bureaucrats for writing rules that few can understand and for placing the force of the entire government against an individual or small business for any infraction of their mandates. We also know bureaucrats for their incompetence in not being able to use their massive resources to prevent large-scale pilfering of our money, such as in the many bank scandals, large-scale corporate fraud, depleted pension funds, and billions of dollars in wasted expenditures. But the bureaucrat is not a bad person. Rather, the bureaucrat is the action arm of the administrative state, and there can be no kakistocracy without bureaucrats at the table.

Let's meet the collabortakers.

1. *Lobbyists* are those citizens whose job it is to persuade Congress, the president, or the bureaucrats to do some-

thing for them. They are merely "hired guns" who are paid to get results for those who hire them, nothing more and nothing less. Many people view lobbyists as corrupt and corrupting our system of government, but in fact the lobbyist is the most honest of all collabortakers. The lobbyist registers with the federal government for all to see what he or she is seeking from the government and how much money he or she is paid to obtain favors or favorable treatment from the government. The lobbyist tells whomever he or she is trying to persuade what he or she wants and why the government official should do it.

While we the American people may not appreciate the work of lobbyists, it is work sanctioned by the First Amendment of our Constitution, which protects their right to associate with and petition our government for whatever grievances they may seek to redress or benefits they may seek to secure. Lobbyists know what their masters want, tell our government what monies or special advantages they want from the nation, and get paid by the beneficiaries of their work. The best interests of the nation are not relevant to the lobbyist, and neither should they be relevant. The lobbyist is hired to get results, and the more the lobbyist can secure for his or her master in terms of money or advantage over others, the more successful the lobbyist is. Finally, the lobbyist also provides benefits to the kakistocrats in the form of campaign contributions, information to help a political ally or harm a political opponent, and lucrative jobs for kakistocrats in the future for doing a good job when in government.

2. *"Friends" of the kakistocrats* are usually former government officials; highly paid executives or former executives of a corporation, union, or trade association; or present or former business associates of government officials from whom they are seeking favors or some special treatment. Many so-called friends are not registered lobbyists; they do not

disclose their actions or requests, and they seek favor based on relationship without any justification. Their conversations with our government officials usually take place in secret personal meetings that are not deemed lobbying by the meeting parties, yet that is where the significant decisions take place.

These "friends" are often the real power behind the throne the kakistocrats sit on. Their power is exercised invisibly, but it profoundly shapes the direction of the kakistocracy. Publicly, the friends seem to be as important as they believe themselves to be. They are important enough to have limousine drivers, eat at the best restaurants, belong to the best clubs, travel to the best resorts, drink the best wine, live in fine houses, employ full-time publicists, send their kids to the best colleges, and live lives based not on knowledge but on connections. And what demonstrates their true ingenuity is that most of their lavish lifestyle is paid for by someone else (corporations, unions, nonprofits, or the taxpayer). But in the final analysis, it is the "friends" who whisper their wants into the ears of the kakistocrats. These never-disclosed meetings have far more impact than the billions of dollars spent by lobbyists to influence government. These "friends" honestly believe they are entitled to receive benefits from the kakistocracy, because they are self-important people.

3. *Corporations* are entities created by statute to limit the liability of their owners, whose goal is asserted to be generating wealth for its investors.

A corporation has been deemed to be a "person" under the law, a fiction created so that it can act in ways a person would act, such as entering into contracts, buying and selling property, making investments, suing and being sued, seeking benefits from the government, and lobbying to gain advantage over competitors, customers, citizens, and the government. But unlike a real person, in place of a heart, soul, or conscience that might place some limits on misconduct, the corporation has a massive legal structure that shields the owners from harm caused by its operations.

Corporations have little concern for workers or communities, or even our nation. They operate wherever and however they can profit the most; that is their objective. Being impersonal and uncaring, the corporation can be used by the management controlling it to scheme and manipulate, if that is believed to be in its best interest. The corporation is only as good as those controlling it, and with few exceptions, those controlling corporations have only one goal: to benefit themselves and, incidentally, their investors.

Corporations technically are controlled by boards of directors that oversee management. While the board of directors retains ultimate legal control of the corporation, management selects friends to make up the board. This gives management the real control over the corporation and its wealth. Friends sit on the boards of companies run by friends. This enables the management to be lavishly compensated even during times of poor performance. In essence, corporate management is an exclusive exchange club that provides rarified status for members and management, consisting of immense compensation packages, luxurious office suites, palatial dining rooms, personal bodyguards, private planes, and chauffeurs. Many leaders of these large corporations surround themselves with people who possess a one-word vocabulary, "yes," and who bestow cult status on them. These leaders, like the pope, are infallible within his or her sphere of control; when poor decisions occur or there is illegal conduct, there is always a lower person paid far in excess of his or her worth to be the fall guy.

With such accumulated power, corporations seek largesse from kakistocrats. They use government regulations as a barrier to limit competition, and they recognize that manipulation of the policies set by the kakistocracy is an easier path to wealth accumulation than competing in the market by producing a great product. The most one can hope for from a corporation is that the actions taken by management for the greatest personal profit will provide some benefit to investors and jobs for Dutiful Cogs.

4. *Political action committee (PAC)* is a general term that includes entities that collect money from collabortakers who want something from the kakistocracy and use the money to influence the kakistocracy into doing what they want. Depending on the structure of the entity receiving the money, some of the money comes from donors who must be identified in political advertisements, whereas some entities, like trade associations, do not have to identify those who contribute the money that pays for the advertisement. These political messages run under the name of the trade association. Limited amounts of money can be given to candidates, whereas an unlimited amount of the money collected can be used to promote the beliefs of the PAC and their chosen candidates.

    These political advertisements are run by organizations with a direct financial or policy stake in the outcome. PACs simply operate in the open-air buying and selling of political candidates and national policies. It is a democratic debate if one has the money to participate in the debate; otherwise, it is merely political product advertisement. In simple terms, all this political speech is free speech for those wealthy enough to inflict their propaganda on us. In polite society, these political activities are termed "voter education."

    The point is that PACs do nothing different from any other advertiser. They sell their goods to the American people in order to generate power and profit for themselves by influencing the kakistocracy.

5. *Unions*—and there are a lot of them: industrial, federal, state and local government unions, as well as unions for teachers, nurses, janitorial services, and many more—all seek to secure immediate benefits from the kakistocracy without any concern for the sector they operate in or the future job prospects of its members or our nation. Historically, the purpose of a union was for workers to band together to achieve better bargaining power for themselves with their employers, so as to enhance their skills, working conditions, and pay. Certainly, that is a good free-market motive. But over time, unions morphed into a corporate structure, with the union boss and the union board becoming like a corporate board, namely, friends protecting friends for their own benefit. The union member, the employee, is only needed for his or her dues.

Compounding the negative actions that forced major industries to declare bankruptcy or move abroad, the unions, in an effort to create powerful coalitions to enhance their power, join forces with groups such as the environmental community, which are opposed to the building of new industries or facilities and the creation of wealth generally. While these partnerships directly cost union membership millions of well-paying jobs, the partnerships do enhance the perceived power of the labor leaders.

As private-sector union membership shrank dramatically over the decades, well-paying jobs in key industries were lost, and displaced workers took lower-paying non-union jobs. This is not a prescription for success, so the unions expanded into sectors where the American public pays the full bill for outrageous demands. The result is a huge growth of public-sector unions. Now, with the United States in trillions of dollars of debt, government unions will face the same difficulties as private-sector unions; union members will be working for a sector that does not have the funds to pay the high costs. At the municipal level, the government entities can go bankrupt. Although the federal government can print money as if it has no consequence, it does so at the peril of the nation. As with the private-sector unions, these government unions will eventually lose many of the well-paying jobs as the government reduces services as part of debt reduction. Meanwhile, the union bosses have few ideas for incentivizing growth in the nation; therefore, unions look to the kakistocracy to protect their jobs and create new ones.

6. *Social-engineering activists* believe themselves to be omniscient and the only segment of society capable of establishing the proper master-servant relationship between themselves and us. These activists comprise thousands of righteous-thinking groups that scare us into believing our wealth and lifestyle are killing the planet and that we need to immediately repent by abandoning all that civilization has brought us. These groups assemble to occupy our streets and to picket, threaten, and boycott our businesses to change their focus from wealth creation to wealth destruction and redistribution.

    These activists use lawsuits to delay or prevent the building of new projects, from an energy facility to a big-box store to a cell tower. These groups seek to have the kakistocracy mandate the type of energy we use, the kind of food we eat, the packaging of the products we buy, the transportation we ride, what land is acceptable for development, and the businesses that are good and bad. These activists demand that the kakistocracy impose mandates on many aspects of economic activity. Of course, the activists would then supervise compliance with the mandates.

7. *Trade associations* are groups of businesses that organize for purposes related to their area of economic activity. The usual types of activities conducted by trade associations are lobbying, electing political candidates, setting standards, and holding social events. There are thousands of these

entities, ranging from Chambers of Commerce to organizations in specific industries such as chemicals, steel, and cement and smaller sectors such as funeral homes, geology, and bakeries, to name a few. Trade associations are scattered throughout the country. The largest trade associations have significant amounts of money and are able to raise even larger amounts of money from their members to influence the kakistocracy, if needed. The trade associations' efforts are to ensure that their members remain nameless when the association persuades the kakistocracy to grant the wishes of its members. As such, trade associations can operate as huge money-laundering machines to influence the kakistocracy without the kakistocracy or the public knowing the identity of who is controlling the association.

The leaders of trade associations prove their skill at laundering political money by deploying large amounts of association resources into selling a public image of themselves as possessing vast knowledge of and political power over the kakistocracy. To solidify their image, they also pick friends as members of their boards and closest advisors, to avoid honest criticism. They travel on private planes, receive huge compensation packages, hire publicists, and bask in the publicity generated not by ideas, of which they have few, but by the efforts of their communications departments to promote them as persons of real power. The power of trade associations in the kakistocracy is image, not content. This is a highly successful undertaking as the kakistocracy treasures followers.

8. *Think tanks* are certainly tanks as we might think of in a war; that is, they are rigid structures capable of holding people and designed to attack. The "tank" part certainly dominates the "think" part of the name. These institutions are organized to produce propaganda for kakistocrats and collabortakers. Unlike trade associations, think tanks pro-

duce the "intellectual" thought products needed by the kakistocracy as support for its actions. Mostly, however, think tanks produce ideas that are the weapons for warring kakistocrats. Unfortunately, by generally producing ideas for a limited group of patrons and kakistocrats, their thinking is somewhat limited. Think tanks do not receive the massive amounts of funding that trade associations receive, but that is understandable, as rehashed ideas are worth less to donors than political attack ads, political contributions, or lobbying. But their ideas are essential, since they are the bullets in the policy debate ground game.

9. *Communicators* are television and radio personalities, print media, public relations firms, publicists, and commentators all working to persuade the public of the truth of their assertions. Some people call these communications "spin," others call it reporting, and still others view it as propaganda for the kakistocrats they support. Some would classify the communications as an extension of the political party supported by the communicator. No matter what the communications are called, the communicators produce constant chatter that bombards us every second of the day. There is so much chatter that it is impossible to separate fact from fiction. There is no longer "real news" or "fake news"; there is just meaningless chatter.

    Those with the money can pump out more chatter. But in the end, there is such a massive amount of chatter being generated that it drowns out ideas that could make a difference. Decades ago, we were told that "the medium is the message." Today, chatter is the message. Yes, these communicators produce infinite amounts of chatter that flow through every aspect of existence, making us confused and numb to the world we occupy. Chatter blocks our vision, infects our brains, and affects our immune system so that we become more susceptible to ugliness of thought and action. That is the goal of communicators—to drive knowledge, reason, and perspective out of society so their form of kakistocracy can dominate all that is left of society. Chatter; nothing but chatter.

10. *Political parties* are nothing more than associations of individuals and wealthy contributors organized to achieve a political goal—control of the kakistocracy. And organized they are! They have been so successful at keeping competition out of the political process by passing overly restrictive election laws that the two political parties literally decide who can participate in the kakistocracy.

There are two major political parties in the kakistocracy, Republican and Democratic. They argue vociferously that they are different and want to take the nation on different paths, but in reality, they have both taken the nation down the same path of massive debt, programs that the nation cannot afford, dysfunctional government, few successful programs, and little hope that things will get better. As long as they can keep competition from forming a new political party, the kakistocracy will continue.

*****

Absent from the discussion of who controls the kakistocracy is the Dutiful Cog, who is most likely at work, creating wealth and keeping the engines of the economy going.

Part I

How It Is

How It Is

The combination of the spirit of the American people, a limited constitutional government, the vast resources of the continent, and a continuous ability to explore, innovate, and change produced what many believe to be the most exceptional nation in human history. This combination allowed its citizens unrivaled personal and political freedom and an ability to create unimaginable wealth for themselves and the nation; it instilled in citizens a firm belief that their country will be greater tomorrow than today; and it fostered a dream in people around the world that if they could just come to the United States of America and participate in our country, we would all have a better future. This is how it was!

"How it is" describes a political system that has broken the ties of trust between those who govern our nation and the citizens who run the engine of America every day by performing the essential functions of working, raising families, building communities, and paying taxes. The kakistocracy is burying the American spirit in massive debt and a vast, incomprehensible set of laws, regulations, taxes, and unfunded liabilities, so that we the people are losing our desire to innovate, build new industrial complexes, create wealth, compete in the world, and, most important, continue regenerating our American spirit.

If we continue on this path, we will ensure the decline of our republic. It will die not from enemy attacks but from the hammering of a gavel wielded by a kakistocrat and by preachers of hate and resentment. This is how it is!

The Kakistocrats Have Forgotten Their Oaths

Every elected member of Congress, every executive and judicial officer of the federal government and of the states takes an oath to support the Constitution of the United States. This oath applies to every person who has freely sought an honored role in the management of our government.

Article VI of the US Constitution states:

> The Senators and Representatives before mentioned, and the Members of the several State Legislatures, and all executive and judicial officers, both of the United States and the several States, shall be bound by Oath or Affirmation, to support this Constitution.

The Constitution sets out a very clear structure for governing. It establishes separate but equal legislative, executive, and judicial branches of government. Each branch has specific powers and responsibilities. Each branch is to be a check on the other branches, so that each one operates within the specific powers given to it under our Constitution. All officials take the oath of office, swearing to fulfill their constitutional duty to the office they serve. One of those duties is to be a check on the excessive or overreaching actions of the other branches of government. Ensuring that every official in every branch works as a check on the other branches is an essential responsibility of our government officials. Without all branches of our government constantly holding in check the powers of the other branches, there is the real and likely possibility that one branch will so intrude on the others as to eliminate our system of checks and balances. And once that is eliminated, the rights of the citizens are eliminated.

Yes, of course, these many government officials would all strongly argue that their every thought, word, and deed is a fulfillment of that oath. Yet it is the very conduct of these officials over many decades that has established a continuing breach of their oath. Amassing trillions of dollars in debt for future generations to repay, operating for years without a budget, allowing unauthorized laws to remain in force without the slightest concern or oversight for decades, allowing hundreds of thousands of regulations to be imposed upon us by unelected bureaucrats who have been delegated power by elected members of Congress who have not read the regulations, funding numerous undeclared wars, and ignoring massive deception in financial markets are but a few of the actions that would not have occurred had the kakistocrats remembered their oath, which requires each branch of government to act as a check on the excesses of the other branches.

To further insult us, it can be safely argued that not one member of the legislative branch has ever read all the legislation he or she voted on, or even a small fraction of the regulations we are forced to live under or be punished should we violate any of them. While our legal system presumes that all citizens know the law for the purpose of punishment should we violate it, citizens know for certain that the kakistocrats do not know the law or the regulations they impose on us.

Unfortunately, the kakistocrats confuse faithfulness to political parties with faithfulness to the Constitution. The term "political party" is not a term in the Constitution. Political parties are merely associations (corporations) that have the same rights as any other organization, and no more. As associations, political parties are merely special interest organizations established to control our government, so the members of the respective party can rule us.

As part of their control effort, the two major parties, actively manipulate the voting system to limit access to the ballot by political third parties with different viewpoints, so they can't compete for control of our government. To gain such control over the voting process, these two major political parties finance and work to elect persons who have the desire to make and execute laws that are promoted by the political party that helped elect them. Once those candidates are elected to run the country, they can appoint thousands of their supporters to positions that impose regulations on us and interpret what our laws mean when applied to us. It is expected that the elected and appointed kakistocrats will implement the policies of the political party that helped them obtain power, while ignoring their true responsibility to act as a check on the other branches of government.

It is precisely because these kakistocrats place loyalty to the political party above loyalty to the branch of government in which they serve that they breach their oath to uphold the Constitution. This is unforgivable as our system of institutional checks and balances is replaced only with the checks imposed by special interest groups, whose sole intent is to place control of our government in the hands of persons loyal to one of the two major political parties. This diminishes the institutions established by the Constitution and the protections it is intended to provide.

The Kakistocrats Have Rewritten the US Constitution

Our founders formed a representative republic. We have formed a kakistocracy. Our founders risked their lives, so we could live in freedom. We have burdened future generations with massive debt, so we can live in comfort. Our founders formed a government that had a responsibility to its citizens. We have a government that is placing our republic at risk. Our Constitution provides for the people to elect a Congress that enacts the laws of the nation. We have allowed the unelected bureaucratic members of the kakistocracy to assume the legislative function of our government. And now Congress is unable to reclaim these legislative functions from the executive branch.

How has this occurred? A brief answer is that each branch of government has, for its own selfish purposes, manipulated the constitutional duties assigned to it. Congress delegated away its legislative authority to the bureaucracy, so it could avoid making difficult political decisions. The executive branch and its huge bureaucracy collect and use all the power it can amass, including legislative power through regulation, so it can achieve maximum control of the country through executive orders, regulations, and enforcement activities. The courts assume legislative power in several ways. While they lack lawmaking power, a military, or the ability to appropriate monies, the courts have great control over legislative policy making by issuing sweeping policy pronouncements, for example, an action is a tax rather than a violation of the Commerce Clause of the Constitution (upholding the Affordable Care Act), or an action is a violation of due process rather than a protection of the national security of the nation (striking down immigration executive orders).

In our present-day kakistocracy, Congress, the nation's constitutionally authorized lawmaker, has lost control of the legislative process to regulatory agencies that continuously interpret, amend, expand, or ignore the laws. The courts have strongly supported this shift by first approving the power of Congress to delegate legislative functions to agencies and recognizing the agencies' right to legislate as part of the rule-making process and then by deferring to agency decisions, since the courts view them as experts when they legislate by rule-making. Neither the delegation of legislative authority to agencies nor the granting of judicial deference to bureaucratic decisions is a power found in the US Constitution. These powers exist only because the courts find them to exist, and this has successfully established agencies as the primary legislative body in the kakistocracy. Agencies will remain in this control position until the courts restrain their decision-making or Congress finds a way to reclaim use of its legislative authority.

Compounding this loss of coequal status is the fact that in a divided government, Congress, unable to reclaim its constitutional powers by enacting new legislation, cannot act as a unified institution, as the loyalty of its individual members is to the political party they represent, not the institution of Congress. Under these conditions, the executive branch and its bureaucracy are safe from challenge. It is unlikely that the political party not controlling the executive branch can secure enough votes from the party controlling it to pass a law with the veto-proof majority needed to restore to Congress the powers given to it by the Constitution. Therefore, through the bureaucracy, the executive branch continues to legislate through the use of regulations, which are generally approved by the courts.

But the most troubling of all the facts is that Congress has abandoned other powers that would allow it to regain its rightful place in our constitutional system. Specifically, Congress authorizes most laws for a period of years and funds them usually on an annual basis. The purpose of authorizing laws for a set period of time is to ensure that Congress has oversight of the laws, to ensure that they work as intended. At the end of the authorized time period, Congress can reauthorize a law, amend it, or let it lapse. Such oversight provides Congress with the ability to address changed circumstances. Moreover, by continuously reviewing the need for a law at the end of its authorized period, Congress retains control over both the laws that are passed and the nation's purse, which funds implementation of the laws. However, Congress, in its continuous attempt to make itself irrelevant, has not regularly performed this oversight and reauthorization function. Instead of letting expired laws lapse or amending unworkable laws to make them workable, Congress merely passes resolutions deeming all expired laws reauthorized, and then funds these laws without any serious review. By using this fiction of deeming expired laws as reauthorized, Congress continuously cedes more and more legislative power to the executive branch and its agencies.

Under this process, the internal workings of the kakistocracy have, in effect, rewritten the US Constitution. In fact, by deeming expired laws as reauthorized without any oversight or formal reauthorization, Congress has abdicated its power to legislate. Moreover, as long as Congress continues to deem expired statutes as reauthorized and funds the implementation of such statutes, it continues to ratify executive authority over all laws enacted by regulation. Getting to this point involved the collaboration of all branches of government. Yes, Congress abdicated its legislative responsibilities, but the judicial branch also recognized the right of Congress to delegate legislative authority to the executive branch and granted deference to the lawmaking actions of agencies.

This new political structure created by the kakistocracy is not a spellbinding story of great intrigue or massive and ruthless rulers seizing power. Rather, it is nothing more than a story of how great ideas such as the Constitution are changed over time by persons of limited vision, who lack courage but possess an obsession to hold political power.

The Kakistocrats Are Imposing Involuntary Servitude on Us and Our Posterity

Is there a constitutional limit to the amount of debt the kakistocracy can impose on us?

Based on Article I, Section 8, of the US Constitution, Congress can tax us and spend and borrow for what it wants, unless the executive vetoes these congressional actions and the veto is upheld.

Congress avoids the tough decision of having us pay for what it spends through higher taxes by simply borrowing more and more money and passing our debt on to future generations. All it takes is for Congress to pass a joint resolution to increase the statutory limit on the public debt. The resolution reads:

> Resolved by the Senate and House of Representatives of the United States of America assembled, that subsection (b) of section 1301 of title 31, United States Code, is amended by striking out the dollar limitation contained in such subsection and inserting in lieu thereof the amount of money it wants to borrow.

It's easy: Congress votes for the printing of unlimited amounts of money that will be paid off in the future by citizens, many of whom have not even been born. Must we live with these decisions, no matter how burdensome? Is there some point at which the debt imposed upon us by the kakistocracy is so great that we are literally put into involuntary servitude? That is prohibited by Amendment XIII of the US Constitution, which reads:

> *Section 1.* Neither slavery nor involuntary servitude, except as a punishment for crime whereof the party shall have been duly convicted, shall exist in the United States, or any place subject to their jurisdiction.

The debate over rising deficits is generations old. Republicans want lower taxes on the rich, drastic cuts to domestic spending, and greater military spending. Democrats want higher taxes on the rich, more domestic spending, and drastic cuts to the military. This debate has resulted in more spending on everything and more borrowing to pay for what Congress was unwilling to pay for by taxing the present generation.

Debt remained below $1 trillion until 1982, but by 1986 federal debt hit the $2 trillion level; it hit $4 trillion by 1992, $6 trillion by 2002, $16 trillion by 2012, and $20 trillion in 2017. And it is still rising by trillions of dollars every few years, with projections that it will reach $25 trillion in a decade.

On top of our national debt, the nation is committed to spending massive amounts of money to make good on promises to fund Social Security, Medicare, Medicaid, social disability programs, prescription drugs for the elderly, and the liabilities that may arise out of the nation's many insurance programs, from flood insurance to problems with nuclear power plants. While there is little agreement on the amount of this unfunded liability, estimates range from $25 trillion to $125 trillion. Whatever the amount, it is staggering, and unless it is addressed, it will be just more debt to be paid by future generations.

In addition, the nation must pay interest on these trillions of dollars of existing debt. While interest payments in 2015 were approximately $225 billion, carrying a 2.4 percent interest rate, it is a certainty that interest rates will rise in the future to attract purchasers of our growing debt.

A national debt exceeding $21 trillion represents approximately a $61,000 mortgage carried by every citizen of the United States, no matter his or her age. As soon as a person is born, he or she has this $61,000 mortgage imposed, to be paid from future earnings. This debt is more than the 2016 median household income in the United States, which was around $51,272. As the debt of the United States increases, so will the debt of every citizen in the country. For every trillion dollars of new debt, each citizen will be responsible for paying another $3,000. Just increasing the debt from its current $21 trillion to the estimated $25 trillion will increase each citizen's debt by $12,000. At the current rate of increase, a child born today with a $61,000 debt could find him- or herself owing hundreds of thousands of dollars of debt at the end of his or her life. At what point does such a debt place the child, our citizen, into involuntary servitude?

To put the magnitude of our $21 trillion debt in perspective, the total value of all companies traded on the US stock market in 2017 was approximately $26 trillion. The value of the assets held by the US government in the form of property, plants, equipment, depreciation, and loans receivable is around $2.7 trillion. The federal government also holds around $3.2 trillion in financial assets; the largest asset being $1.5 trillion in student loan debt, which represents almost half of its financial assets. The federal government also owns approximately six hundred and fifty-one million acres of land, nearly thirty percent of the country, mostly in the western states. Assuming an average value of $8,000 per acre, this land would carry a market value of $5.2 trillion, which brings the total value of US government assets, buildings, equipment, and land to around $11 trillion.

There are many other federal assets that have value, such as two hundred and sixty-one million ounces of gold, which may be worth around $11 billion, and mineral rights and offshore land and energy resources, likely worth in the trillions of dollars, which are part of the balance sheet when considering how the kakistocracy can address the debt burden on citizens. Should some of these assets be used to reduce our debt?

Involuntary servitude refers to compulsory labor to satisfy a debt or peonage, in which the debtor must work for his creditor until the debt is paid off. In general, involuntary servitude is not considered to be any work or service that forms the normal obligations of the citizenry of a self-governing country. Under this interpretation, the kakistocracy argues that spending, taxing, and borrowing are merely the normal activities of government. If true, then there is no limit to the amount of debt a government can impose on its citizens. But is this an idea sanctioned by our Constitution?

The imposition of massive debt by one generation on future generations is stealing. The imposition of such massive amounts of debt upon citizens that they or their descendants are not able to pay off in their lifetime is not promoting the general welfare or securing the blessings of liberty for posterity. Binding the rewards of each citizen's labor to the repayment of debt incurred by the kakistocracy at some point becomes involuntary servitude. While paying reasonable taxes may be the price of living in a free society, there is a point at which the imposition of massive debt on all citizens forces them into involuntary servitude. The only real question is, at what point does the debt imposed upon us convert the social obligation of paying reasonable taxes into involuntary servitude?

Complex Governments Are Corrupt

Tacitus, a Roman senator and historian of the Roman Empire, observed: "The more corrupt the state, the more numerous the laws." This simple observation captures the essence of how the kakistocracy uses laws and regulations to capture control of citizens, plunder our treasure, drain the energy of the nation, and leave the Dutiful Cogs to carry the massive debts of the state on their broad shoulders. While the initial enactment of laws may be just and their administration fair, as more and more laws are enacted, the kakistocrats and collabortakers find ways to use the laws to take from some and give to others, to place protections on some and penalize others, and to provide market access to friends while placing barriers to entry on competitors. All is done in the name of "law-giving." The violation of any law becomes the justification for punishing those deemed to be a threat to the kakistocracy. And when the laws of a state become so numerous as to no longer be understood, it is the kakistocrats who determine what the laws mean and who the violators are.

How does a government expand from a 4,400-word Constitution that sets forth clear but limited governmental powers of divided responsibilities to ensure checks on each branch of government into a massive administrative state?

The multiplication of laws does not occur by accident; it occurs as Congress passes broad, vague laws that most members have not read. The bureaucrats then implement these broad, vague laws by imposing hundreds of thousands of regulations on us. And yes, regulations are laws. Under this process, almost every act of the kakistocracy produces new laws, and laws beget laws, until there are so many that we are crushed by the laws that impose conditions on us of which we are not aware. To illustrate this point, Congress has passed so many laws, the experts cannot determine how many there are. These laws are then administered by federal agencies that have issued more than two hundred thousand rules to implement them. These rules are further explained by hundreds of thousands of pages of guidance and opinion letters. Violation of any requirement in any regulation can result in administrative, civil, or criminal charges brought by any of tens of thousands of agency-employed enforcement officers.

In short, the administrative state is so massive, so complex, that we are all criminals, and we do not know it. Every day we are likely to break some law, and though we may not get caught, we will get caught should a kakistocrat be unhappy with our conduct, no matter how slight the deviation from the mandates of the administrative state.

The courts also legislate. Clear-cut examples abound as courts expand law without additional legislation. The National Environmental Policy Act is a simple, six-page statute requiring federal agencies to evaluate the environmental impacts of federal decisions and set forth options to protect the environment. Over time, the courts, not Congress, expanded the reach of this law by mandating that every aspect of harm to the environment, no matter how insignificant, be evaluated by every federal agency that might have some impact on the activity being reviewed. Subsequently, the courts, not Congress, allowed environmental groups to bring suit to ensure that every environmental review sufficiently addresses every environmental concern, no matter how insignificant. And while the courts were expanding the reach of the law, so was the agency administering it.

Just this simple set of court decisions converted a simple statute that required federal agencies to consider environmental consequences into perhaps the most onerous task in government, requiring tens of thousands of pages of review for decisions by federal agencies involving the environment. By expanding this simple law, the kakistocrats on the courts legislated, and those legislative enactments now are used to significantly delay any major federal decision, no matter how important the project is to the nation. When the courts take these legislative actions, the Constitution is minimized, and power is redistributed outside of its framework.

Another difficulty in the present legal morass is the question of whether all these laws can even be properly administered. If they cannot be properly administered, is not the mere clutter of these laws harmful to the proper and efficient management of a civil society? As the sheer number of laws and their complexity increase, our country is squandering precious resources as it focuses on so many activities that we lose sight of our larger goal, the freedom of our people to take different paths to achieving personal goals, wealth, innovation, and knowledge. Every unneeded law and regulation cuts off some of our freedom, depletes our resources, and ties us to a path determined by a kakistocrat who is not likely to understand the consequences of his or her actions.

So why do we let the kakistocrats rule? Why do we hire millions of them? Why do we pay them more than we get paid ourselves? How did this happen? Why do we let it continue?

Simply, this is what happens in a kakistocracy. It is the logical outcome when members of Congress do not read or understand what they are legislating and are more concerned about being reelected than upholding their oath to the Constitution. It is the logical outcome when the executive branch worries more about accumulating power than taking care that the laws are faithfully executed. It is the logical outcome when courts interpret laws so as to implement the political objective of the jurist writing the opinion. It is the logical outcome when collabortakers organize to take as much benefit as the kakistocracy will give them.

With hundreds of thousands of pages of laws, regulations, guidance, opinions, and orders, the kakistocrats and the collabortakers benefit from a system in which there is no transparency in the actions of government. And when a government is not transparent, it is arbitrary! And when a government is too complex, it is corrupt!

The Kakistocrats Are Regulating Our Nation Out of Business and the New Sheriff Can't Stop It!

The amount of regulation was a significant part of the 2016 presidential election debates. The Democrat praised regulations as protecting everything from the planet to the child with asthma. The Republican strongly argued that regulations cost thousands of jobs, shuttered industries, and destroyed communities. The Republican won, and immediately after being sworn into office, the new president unleashed a torrent of executive orders instructing agencies to review, amend, or rescind a large number of regulations, and he approved fourteen Congressional Review Act resolutions of disapproval, which repealed regulations issued at the end of the prior administration. Good start at breaking up the kakistocracy, but such actions will have little impact on a regulatory structure that has hundreds of thousands of regulations and many more thousands of guidance documents, opinion letters, and agency orders that form the foundation of the kakistocracy and govern almost every aspect of our lives. No person, not even the president, can dismantle the kakistocracy without the full consent of the kakistocracy or a full-scale electoral revolt of the Dutiful Cogs.

Kakistocrats and collabortakers have so intertwined their laws and regulations that the structure of our government is almost impossible to disassemble. In fact, it is harder to take the regulatory structure apart than it is to put it together. Putting the regulatory structure together merely requires a kakistocrat to propose a regulation, pretend to listen to public comment, and issue a final rule that a court will usually find rational, or if the regulation is questionable, the court will usually defer to the expertise of the agency. That is all that a kakistocrat needs do to impose a regulation, which functions as a law.

Taking the regulatory state apart, however, requires repealing laws and regulations. Repealing a law requires Congress and the president acting together, or Congress having a supermajority of votes to overcome a presidential veto. This is an extremely high bar to meet, so it is very likely that the laws will remain in place, and we will be subject to them should the executive want to enforce them against us.

Repealing an existing regulation requires significant time and effort. The agency repealing an existing rule of a prior administration must explain why it wants to change course and why the repeal of the rule is reasonable. After the proposed repeal of the prior administration's rule is finalized, the interest groups seeking to preserve the rule will sue. The kakistocrats serving as judges will review the final rule to ascertain whether a reasonable decision maker (the judge) would respond to the facts in the same manner as the agency seeking to repeal an already issued rule. The judge holds the power to determine which of the competing agency interpretations of the rule is correct.

What is troubling being that Congress, our primary lawmaking body and author of the law being interpreted, has relinquished any say in the outcome since it generally delegates authority to the agency to fill in any blanks when a law is broad or vague, a common occurrence. Moreover, since Congress lacks a strong capacity to perform oversight over agency regulations; a vacuum is created that allows the agency to determine what the rule means and for the judiciary to determine if the agency's determination is correct. Congress, the lawmaker is out of the decision-making process unless it can enact a new law to overturn what it believes to be a wrong interpretation of the regulation or it is able to use the Congressional Review Act to repeal a regulation it does not like, a task which is only available for use in a limited, legislatively established, time-period.

In the course of a full President's term the agency usually follows the President's direction on regulatory matters and Congress watches from the sidelines. However, when there is a change in administrations as we had in 2017, and the new administration wants to change the regulations issued by the prior administration, difficulties arise. The new administration cannot just direct the agency to repeal regulations it does not like; rather it must go through the same process to repeal a rule as the agency undertook to develop and implement a rule.

This effort requires the new administration to provide the public with notice of the rule change and allow the public to comment on it. This process is time consuming but it also allows the agency the time to develop reasons that persuade a reviewing court that it has a rational basis for repealing or amending a regulation that the prior administration issued by establishing it was rational.

The administrative process becomes disconcerting at this point since the old and the new administrations have completely different views of the same law passed by Congress. One administration believes that law passed by Congress gives it authority to impose a massive new regulatory agenda while the new administration believes that the same statutory language does not require any regulation or minimal regulation at best. A good example of this conflict is when the Obama administration interpreted the Clean Water Act to require the federal government to regulate almost all waterbodies from rivers to ponds to ditches. The Trump administration believed regulations issued under the Clean Water Act could only impact waterbodies that involved interstate commerce, i.e. rivers or large waterbodies.

The same law is being implemented by different administrations with diametrically opposed meanings and outcomes. How can the same law, in a short period of time, without any congressional action, have opposite meanings? While the court will determine what it believes is the correct interpretation of the law, the situation points out how much authority agencies and courts have in lawmaking.

The situation also underscores the difficulty of dramatically shrinking the administrative state since each regulatory change requires an extensive effort to establish a rational policy that can persuade a court to approve a completely contrary interpretation of a law.

The new sheriff might be able to change a few of the regulations, maybe even fifty or up to a few hundred during a four-year term but it will not have the resources or time to change the administrative state that is comprised of over two hundred thousand regulations that have been put in place over the last seventy years. Simply, the Administrative State stays in place unless Congress can reclaim its legislative authority by placing limits on agency and judicial discretion or by repealing the laws that require the regulations be issued. It is for this reason that Congress must act to reclaim its legislative authority. Changing this situation will require Congress to pass a regulatory reform law that limits agency discretion in the rule-making process, establishes clear standards for evidence needed as a foundation for issuing a final regulation and prohibits the courts from freely granting deference to agency decisions. Until this happens, the administrative state stays firmly in place.

The Kakistocracy Is a Political Soundstage Managed by Scarecrows

No two images could better capture the essence of life in the kakistocracy than the soundstage and the scarecrow. A soundstage is a soundproof platform for recording and broadcasting voices and producing television shows and advertisements, which are nothing more than series of filmed images viewed in sufficiently rapid succession to create the illusion of motion and continuity. The scarecrow is a straw-filled decoy, made in the shape of a person, designed to scare but without a brain and totally incapable of action. Through the use of these two devices, the kakistocracy has literally turned management of our government into a movie script designed to scare us if we do not give it what it wants.

In the kakistocracy, the soundstage is the structure where a kakistocrat's image is molded by scarecrow collabortakers, using polling data to finely craft the public statements and visuals that develop the kakistocrat's brand, and projecting onto the public an almost infinite number of discrete pieces of information connected only by spin. While the outside voices of Dutiful Cogs cannot be heard inside the soundstage, the kakistocracy launches its propaganda in many forms, including press statements, speeches, videos, books, advertisements, blogs, e-mails, and tweets. These statements are intended to inform the public of its actions. But in reality, the kakistocrat only makes these statements to sound active and important. To the Dutiful Cogs, the sounds uttered by the kakistocracy do not conform to the reality of their existence, which the kakistocracy views as insignificant. The sounds they hear from the kakistocrat are huffing and puffing that signify nothing.

The constant news cycle, the unlimited chatter of cyberspace, and the collabortakers' spin continuously feed the ego of the kakistocrat, giving him or her a stuffed sense of primordial influence on the actions of the day. The kakistocrat believes every word of the spin.

To sound powerful, the kakistocrat delivers chattering lectures with high-sounding titles like "the State of the Union," "the State of American Business," "the State of US Energy," "the State of the Environment," the state of whatever the kakistocrat wants us to believe important. Kakistocrats view themselves as leaders of important matters, of great influence and brilliance, understanding the ills of the nation and possessing great insight into human foibles. In essence, the spin becomes ultimate reality to the kakistocrat, and the kakistocrat constantly searches for a parade that he can jump in front of and claim to be leading. This is life in a kakistocracy for those of us who are idle enough to pay attention to the soundstage from which the kakistocrat speaks, based on the scarecrows' advice.

The scarecrows work tirelessly on the production of the kakistocrat's image. They constantly do press statements on behalf of the kakistocrat, announcing every thought as the path forward to saving the democracy. The scarecrow toils, writing high-sounding speeches that contain little substance while living in fear that the kakistocrat might go off script and invite inspection of the political soundstage. This fear drives the development of vague statements that spark little disagreement by allowing enough wiggle room to ensure that the kakistocrat's view can always be justified, or at least reasonably explained. To achieve this verbal nirvana, the scarecrow tests every message, worries about every foe, and shuns any provocative or novel thought that actually might point to a path for addressing the issues. Output from the soundstage is solely a script that attempts to manipulate the reality we live in.

And recently scarecrows started using a form of communication called "tweeting," which allows anyone to broadcast short (up to two hundred and eighty characters) text messages to the world. There are billions of tweets being inflicted on the world. The producers of these tweets hope that someone, somewhere on earth finds their constant stream of brain farts worthy of being read and responded to. But to the kakistocrat, a tweet is a needed pronouncement to his or her followers, who are so important to his or her ego that the scarecrows actively purchase twitter followers so as to announce a high number of them, thereby signifying the importance of the kakistocrat. In the world of tweets, followers demonstrate importance, even purchased followers, while substance and analysis are abandoned and derided.

On a daily basis, the scarecrows know that the kakistocrat needs to see his or her name in print or be heard on television uttering some banal four-second phrase that has absolutely no impact on reality other than the reality in his or her own head. Such reality, no matter how delusional, is the kakistocrat's only reality.

And then we have the scarecrows bringing us special events like galas, conventions, or large celebrations that highlight what may be a noble undertaking but are solely efforts to make the kakistocrat appear greater than the mortals in attendance. Scarecrows build out the soundstage with large television screens, flags, cameras, banners, and even seals of noted institutions—trappings so regal they would be worthy of a king's coronation. Among these trappings, the scarecrows place the kakistocrat at a podium that is small compared to the room, with massive movie screens on both sides, so the kakistocrat's image dwarfs the room and the listeners. In such circumstances, the kakistocrat looks like a king rising above the mortals in the seats below. All in attendance play their parts as subjects, and the rest of the world moves on.

These activities by the scarecrows to puff up the image of the kakistocrat to the outside world are expensive and performed by people who believe they have the power to reshape reality with hollow statements. But the kakistocrat is not paying these expenses; he or she is using the funds of collabortakers looking for special favors or services or institutions promoting themselves. When image is the only concern, cost, responsibility, and accomplishments become irrelevant.

In essence, life within a kakistocracy is full of hollow scripts that separate the governing and the governed. The American people simply need to understand that in a kakistocracy, it is only the kakisto-crats and collabortakers who matter; all others are insignificant. Only when the American people are face-to-face with the soundstage, and the scarecrows who write the scripts, can they appreciate that those who seek power over us are the very individuals who should never be entrusted with power. Once this reality is understood, we can dis-mantle the soundstage from which the kakistocrat speaks and from which he or she has brought this nation to the brink of economic peril and political sclerosis.

Beware of the Kakistocrats' Dodgery and Jobbery

It does not matter what the crisis or what the situation is; the process of governing is used to advantage the kakistocracy and to disadvantage the Dutiful Cogs. Simply, the kakistocrats make themselves and their collabortakers winners while placing the entire burden of the nation's debt, the harms of war, and the risks of society on the Dutiful Cogs. This has been the situation for at least a century, but in the middle of the twentieth century, the kakistocrats began to firmly understand that their power can grow infinitely larger simply by creating new government programs that reward collabortakers who help them attain and maintain power.

How our nation got into this position can only be described as dodgery and jobbery.

Dodgery is when a person dodges or evades honesty or acts shifty or as a trickster. The skill of dodgery is the essence of the kakistocracy. It is usually learned as one is educated in the ways of becoming a kakistocrat and perfected as one becomes more ensconced in the kakistocracy. The skill requires a willingness to abandon straightforward speech for reliance on polls, so as to understand what citizens might expect from the government. And then, with the obsessive use of focus groups, the kakistocrat learns how to make any statement sound supportive of the position held by almost any group in society. These two devices, polls and focus groups, provide the kakistocrat with the skills needed to remain in power without having to be bound by his or her words. In short, the kakistocrat uses words to mean anything he or she wants them to mean. The kakistocrat's words are used to deceive.

While Dutiful Cogs worry about job, family, friends, community, and country, the kakistocrats in Congress adopt rules of procedure that allow them to speak with high-sounding language that informs constituents that they voted for whatever the constituents supported. This is done with parliamentary maneuvers that allow kakistocrats to vote for and against the same law. This occurs when there are multiple votes on different parts of the law: there is a vote on final passage, but before that there are opposing amendments. By voting one way on the amendments and another way on final passage, the kakistocrat covers the positions of all voters. This procedure allows the congressional kakistocrat to tell constituents he or she supported their wishes, no matter what those wishes are, thus avoiding significant citizen retribution at the polls.

Another mechanism that allows kakistocrats to make any statement, no matter how it dodges an issue, is when the leadership of Congress refuses to allow votes on particular subjects. This allows the kakistocrat to make any type of statement to constituents without any possibility of being challenged.

The most common trick is when the kakistocrat feigns anger over a policy to gain support from voters. In this instance, the kakistocrat introduces legislation that, if enacted, would address the voters' problem. What voters are not told is that the legislation will never be considered—it is worth less than the paper it is printed on. The legislation was introduced to make the kakistocrat member of Congress appear to be a forceful leader, but the real reason was to deceive and hide the real inaction of the kakistocrat.

Then there are the reforms offered by kakistocrats. The congressional kakistocrats promise that legislation will not go to the floor for a vote without several days' notice. Ostensibly, this is to allow them to read the legislation they are voting on. How many kakistocrats read a two-thousand-page health-care bill or a thousand-page banking bill or a tax bill drafted and negotiated by the leadership in Congress and immediately brought to the floor for a vote? Maybe a few? Kakistocrats promise responsibility and accountability, but they do all they can to avoid assuming actual responsibility or account-ability; that would be too dangerous. So how do kakistocrats justify receiving a paycheck without actually reading the documents they are voting on? They always have an excuse, e.g. the need to avoid a program expiring; or a tight legislative schedule; or it was a leadership decision; or I wasn't on that committee; or I introduced a bill to address that issue. There is always a reason the congressional kakisto-crat is not responsible for his or her promises.

And then there is *jobbery*, which is making private profit out of a public office. Forms of jobbery are in the news every day, and all read the same: common man is elected or appointed to a position of power and uses position for personal benefit. The list reads like a crime blotter, except there is little prosecution, or in many instances, the conduct is actually approved by an ethics panel established by the kakistocrats. A few instances tell us all we need to know.

- Members of Congress direct federal monies to redevelop land in areas they own.
- Federal contracts are directed to foundations established by friends of congressmen, who also make substantial contri-butions to them.
- An advisor lobbies the president to award contracts to a firm represented by the advisor's wife.
- Members of Congress are exempt from insider trading rules.
- Federal funds are used to restore a beach near the vacation home of a member of Congress.
- Members of Congress steer lucrative business to lobbying firms that employ their relatives.
- Members of Congress secure lucrative jobs for their spouses in lobbying, real estate, and finance, where referrals of busi-ness are significant.
- Congress allows hundreds of employees in the kakistocracy to avoid paying federal income taxes or repaying student loans.

- Congress views the admission of a secretary of the treasury that he substantially underreported his federal taxes as a good-faith oversight.
- Federal retirement packages given to regulators are 2.7 times more generous than what is paid by large private-sector firms.

Thanks to jobbery, kakistocrats enter public life with few resources and leave as wealthy people while only being paid the salaries of government officials.

The Kakistocrats Are the Ultimate Special Interest

From the moment one of our citizens voluntarily takes the constitutional oath to serve as a member of Congress or an executive official to manage the affairs of government, or to sit as a judge of others, that person enters a fiduciary relationship with our nation. From that point forward, this fiduciary is under oath to manage our government for the benefit of the governed. Unfortunately, once in power, these ordinary citizens usually morph into kakistocrats, who manage our government for their personal benefit and the benefit of the collabortakers.

When the kakistocrat acts to benefit his or her political career, the political party he or she belongs to, or the collabortakers who helped secure their position, the kakistocrat separates himself or herself from the citizens to be served. Such separation makes it extremely difficult for the kakistocrat to honor the oath to support the Constitution by serving as a check on the other branches of government. Without the continuing checks of the respective branches of government on each other, we cannot preserve our republic. Today, we are in a situation in which control over our government by political parties with agendas that benefit the collabortakers means that the only checks and balances in our system come from the political parties and the collabortakers, not the branches of government, as mandated by our Constitution. This is a political check on power that can change as the kakistocrats find benefits elsewhere.

Although the First Amendment of the US Constitution protects all interest groups through freedom of speech, freedom of assembly, and the right to petition the government for grievances, we must continuously recognize that we now live in a system structured by special-interest groups for the benefit of the kakistocrats and collabortakers. As such, the political parties are nothing more than mere associations of citizens formed to secure special benefits for themselves, the same as any other special interest groups, whether they are Chambers of Commerce, trade or professional associations, social activists, PACs, or any other entity that organizes for the purpose of obtaining benefits from the government for its members.

The big difference, however, between political parties and other special-interest groups is that two political parties, Democratic and Republican, have amassed such great power over the political process that they have been able to impose upon smaller political parties' significant obstacles to having their name appear on the ballot, e.g. requiring a significant number of signatures on nominating petitions. Those laws combined with costly lawsuits challenging the signatures on the nominating petitions of the smaller parties, allow the two major parties to possess a duopoly power over the selection of who will control the kakistocracy. And with such powers the kakistocrats can ensure that they benefit from the actions of the kakistocracy by the following:

- Accepting campaign contributions from individuals who want them to use the nation's treasury to bestow on collabortakers specific benefits from the government in the form of grants, contracts, subsidies, tax credits, privileged status, jobs, and reduced tax rates for the super-rich.
- Drawing congressional districts in a manner that protects them and their collabortakers from challenge.
- Setting congressional compensation, pension, and health benefits at levels substantially more generous than what is received by the vast majority of the American people, awarded no matter how poorly they perform.
- Paying government workforce compensation, pension, and health-care packages far more generous than can be paid in the private sector, regardless of level of performance.

- Using the appropriations process and the monies paid in taxes by the American people to the Treasury of the United States for such purposes as will help with their political reelection.
- Using their positions in government to secure significant wealth when out of office.
- Using their government contacts to help family and friends secure jobs with entities that need benefits from or contracts with the government.
- Aggrandizing their reputations by having buildings, streets, airports, and sometimes even monuments named in their honor.
- Forming charities and social welfare organizations to pass the wealth of the nation to political friends and family while granting special and unnoticed access to decision-makers.
- Bailing out the wealthy when their risky business/banking/investment practices fail.
- Securing valuable inside information that allows them to profit from stocks, land transactions, and other profit-making opportunities.
- Failing, at times, to pay taxes on income received, without any penalty.
- Leaking classified documents to destroy opponents for personal benefit.

And the list goes on, as long as the members of the kakistocracy have access to our assets and manage our government.

In summary, the kakistocrats and their collabortakers are the ultimate special interest groups that take from us to benefit themselves.

Our Republic Will Not End by Invasion but by the Gavel and by Preachers of Hate and Resentment

The United States comprises hundreds of millions of people who love this country, work to take advantage of its opportunities, pray for its success, help their neighbors, and realize every day that we are a great nation. We have weathered wars, depressions, dust bowls, bank failures, unlawful spying, discrimination, and periods of great inhumanity. We have survived, and each challenge has made us stronger. Each challenge has given us the wisdom and the courage to change the wrongs we have committed and the desire to be more just. There is almost no goal we cannot achieve or adversity we cannot conquer if we are together under our Constitution.

The risks we face as a nation will not be from the hands of our enemies, rather the risks we face are from the hands of the kakistocrats wielding the gavels of government and in the strident voices of those who preach hate and resentment as tools to gain further control of the kakistocracy.

The constant pounding of the gavel signifies more laws, more regulations, more complexity, more debt, more wars, more government, more kakistocrats, and a more solidly ensconced kakistocracy. More law means greater control over our lives by the kakistocracy.

But the pounding of the gavel allows the collabortakers to incite hatred and rage throughout the land toward anyone who is different in looks, beliefs, and even political leanings. Listen to news and commentary constantly injected into our lives! The collabortakers, especially the communicators, are the echo chamber of the kakistocracy.

They sound the propaganda of the kakistocrats until it is considered truth by many of our citizens.

As a strong nation, we may have a huge tolerance for a kakistocracy that ignores the attacks on the constitutional rights of citizens, sometimes even for long periods; but eventually the actions of those resentful, hateful people will be too much, and those being attacked will retaliate with equal or greater force. The kakistocracy may condemn the attacks with words, but it will likely stand down and watch the haters attack us, since beating down the Dutiful Cogs increases their power over us.

As the wielders of the gavel and the preachers of hate become more combined as one entity, the kakistocracy experiences massive policy swings, which change the nature of its attacks on the Dutiful Cogs. For years, the kakistocracy, through the use of presidential power, increased its control over us by both increasing and selectively enforcing more and more laws. As the Dutiful Cogs became extremely frustrated over the oppression, they used their votes to elect a president who promised to radically eliminate the excessive regulatory burdens on the nation. As the new president began to eliminate the laws of the past, the similarities between time periods emerged. In both time periods, it was the president, not the Congress, who changed the laws we live under. One changed the laws with "pen and phone," the other with "tweets." Both ways make Congress irrelevant by ignoring the first established power in our Constitution which states— "All Legislative Powers herein granted shall be vested in a Congress of the United States, which shall consist of a Senate and House of Representatives."

The most disconcerting aspect of these changes is that by using massive executive power to change laws without Congress, the next president using the same executive power can also change the laws without Congress. As an absentee legislature, Congress allows the nation to be managed in an arbitrary manner that accepts radical changes of policy by the executive in short periods of time. As the kakistocracy functions in greater uncertainty, it becomes less transparent, less able to act, and accountability is lost. The result is that the Dutiful Cogs become more disconnected from the core beliefs in the Constitution, as the decisions of government are arbitrary, instituted by power, and lacking the rule of law.

Most rational humans understand that we need a government to protect the nation from its enemies and protect and defend our constitutional rights. The issue, therefore, is not over whether to have a federal government; that was settled centuries ago. The issue we face is whether we as citizens have the capability to reclaim management of our government by installing leaders who worry about its citizens. As presently constructed, the kakistocrats have clearly and consistently proven that they cannot manage the complexity they have created or the money they squander trying to build a society that has little accountability for its actions.

Fortunately, providence places destiny in our hands. A few thousand years ago, the philosopher Heraclitus stated that "a man's character is his fate." So, too, for a nation: a nation's character is its fate. With little effort, we can continue with the kakistocrats in control of our fate, or each of us can reach deep inside and pull out what we know to be true: that if we want freedom, protection of our property, opportunity to succeed, justice before the law, and a nation safe from threat, we must exercise our power as citizens and remove the kakistocrats so that we can return to a government of the people, by the people, and for the people. The choice over our destiny rests in our hands. The paths available are divergent, one leading to decline and despotism and the other to freedom. The path to decline and despotism is the easier of the paths; we just need to do nothing, and the kakistocrats will take us there, with promises of gifts but the deliverance of servitude. The path to freedom is the difficult journey. There are no promises of gifts or joy, but there is the knowledge that every action taken by a free person adds to the freedom for all of us to pursue dreams that can only be achieved when a government is controlled by the citizens of the nation under the framework of the Constitution.

Part II

Principles of Federal Governance

Need for a Federal Governance Policy

The kakistocracy controls the levers of power to make and enforce the laws we live under. The exercise of such control is called governing. Those governing us have the political power to literally determine what laws are made, what the laws mean, which laws will be enforced and against whom, and how much of our money will be spent. The only viable check on these political powers is whatever counterforces can be applied by citizens and the respective political branches against the other branches. Without very strong checks and balances in our government, those holding power will rule as they wish, since they will not voluntarily limit their powers.

Compounding the kakistocracy's exercise of power is the fact that there is no standard of conduct or set of principles that guide governing on its most important goal, the long-term success of the nation. In short, unlike corporations that develop aspirational governance processes to attempt to achieve financial oversight, openness, accountability, and transparency in achieving their goals, our government does not have any type of governance process; it only has a political process for governing.

A policy for governing would be similar to corporate governance, in that it would be more than requiring obedience to our laws; it would be a framework of operation established by those in power to guide the management of the government to attain the overall objectives in every aspect of government. Government governance policy is a process beyond power politics; it is a process of respect for the separate powers of the different branches of government and the role of citizens, so as to have a well-managed government whose goal is to achieve a functionally sustainable and successful nation that is accountable, open, and fair to its people.

The clearest illustration of this point is the development of corporate governance. Corporations must obey the laws that govern them. But corporations, after many scandals, developed what is termed "corporate governance," which is a set of rules and best practices that establish a framework for obtaining their goals for all their stakeholders, ranging from shareholders to environmental concerns to the supply chain. It is more than technical compliance with legal requirements. It is a process of cooperating, monitoring, and implementing a set of goals that is established by those with the power to achieve the success of the corporation.

With few exceptions, kakistocrats assert that under our Constitution and laws, their actions fit squarely within the laws of the nation. Technically, they are generally correct, but being correct is irrelevant if their management of the nation is disastrous. What is needed from the kakistocracy is for it to recognize that the government must be operated for the overall good of the nation, not the political benefit of kakistocrats and collabortakers.

To successfully transform the nation from a kakistocracy back to a viable republic, the kakistocracy must collectively align its interests with and be responsible for the long-term success of the nation. To achieve this alignment, a few modest principles are proposed.

Governance Principle 1

Kakistocrats Do Not Have Rights, Only Responsibilities

There is only one principle for governing: the US Constitution. There can be no other way to create a legitimate government. Government cannot be imposed by force, inherited, or created by a few to benefit a few; otherwise it is not government under our Constitution. Since we created our government solely to protect and secure the rights of all Americans, we cannot give it any power to take away the rights or property of some for the benefit of a few, or even the many. All we can do is impose responsibilities on those individuals who freely seek and assume the honor of serving in our government.

Unfortunately, as the government grows in laws and rules, the kakistocracy accumulates power. This power is created by the laws and rules the kakistocrats enact and administer. Each law and rule needs interpretation, and it is the kakistocrats who determine its meaning. After many determinations, the kakistocrats come to believe that the power rests in them, and their exercise of power equates to the exercise of responsibility. Gradually, the kakistocrats exercise these powers against the people and the reverse occurs: government has all the rights, and we the people have only responsibilities to the government. It is time that we the people exercise our rights under the Constitution and that those occupying the kakistocracy assume their constitutionally imposed responsibilities of providing for the common defense and promoting the general welfare, not any specific political welfare or the welfare of the collabortakers. It is time all kakistocrats understand that upon taking the Constitutional oath, they voluntarily assume the responsibility to support and defend our Constitution and that they possess no rights against us other than those we legally allow them to exercise. The voluntarily assumed responsibility cannot be to a political party or to collabortakers, nor can it ever be for personal benefit. Rather, the kakistocrats' responsibility can only be to the Constitution and the American people.

Governance Principle 2

Kakistocrats Must Become Fiduciaries

A fiduciary is a person who has a duty, created by a voluntary undertaking, to act primarily for the benefit of another in matters connected with such undertaking. All kakistocrats voluntarily seek and assume positions in our government and freely take an oath to support the Constitution. When they voluntarily assume the responsibility of managing our government, we entrust them with our money, our property, the fair implementation of our laws, and the defense of our country. These are massive responsibilities that, if not properly executed, can create massive abuses that inflict great harm on our people and nation.

While they occupy the offices of government, we pay the kakistocrats well for their services, but we give them no rights over us other than the duty to manage the government for our benefit. The kakistocrats must act as a fiduciary to us, and should never act for their personal benefit, no matter how low or exalted their position in our government might be. Any conduct for personal or political benefit or the benefit of the collabortakers is a breach of fiduciary duty.

The kakistocrat is never the principal to whom we report but rather the agent who takes orders from us. When kakistocrats deviate from promoting the general welfare by promoting individual, political, or collabortakers' welfare, whether by making grants to corporations, legislating tax advantages to special groups, or administering the law in an unequal manner that benefits the privileged while punishing those not as well connected, they breach their fiduciary duty.

When kakistocrats borrow from the wealth of future generations for the purpose of currying political favor from collabortakers or other kakistocrats, they violate their oath to the Constitution by ensuring the involuntary servitude of future generations. And this servitude will break the links that form the continuity of society between generations. Once these generational links are broken by this breach of fiduciary duty, the kakistocrats break the nation.

Governance Principle 3

The Privileges of the Kakistocracy Must Be Abolished

Since the kakistocrats as fiduciaries have no rights, only responsibilities to the nation they serve, all privileges they have taken for themselves must be abolished.

The elected kakistocrats in Congress determine their salaries and pensions, which laws apply to them or which ones they are exempted from, and what money they can receive from their campaign supporters, and they possess the ability, through gerrymandering, to influence the process that allows them to select who will elect them, so they can serve at their pleasure.

The executive kakistocrat lives in the largest and most opulent public housing project in the nation, the White House. The executive is surrounded by servants and valuable antiques, given an almost unlimited expense account, and able to use expensive aircraft to travel anywhere, including vacations, golfing trips, and political events deemed as government business, or just tours of the Statute of Liberty or trips to personal resorts. Whatever the executive's desire, it is satisfied, and the people of the nation pay for it, not only while the executive is in office, but for the executive's remaining lifetime.

The judicial kakistocrats occupy buildings of great architecture containing finely finished rooms that citizens only see when seeking to protect their rights or defend themselves from the power of the government. These judicial kakistocrats are the final interpreters of our Constitution, which gives them great power to determine what the Constitution and laws mean at any one time. They are appointed for life, receive a salary for life, and are rarely questioned by any member of the public or the press. In short, this is the only part of the kakistocracy that can give deference to its own opinions and determine the limits of its own power.

And then there are the kakistocrats who make up the bureaucracy and sit in those hundreds of federal buildings in Washington, DC, and across the country. It is this part of the kakistocracy that takes in and distributes the money of the nation and writes and implements the hundreds of thousands of laws and regulations that are so complex that no human can know how to comply with more than a very small number of them. As federal bureaucrats, these kakistocrats are far more likely to die on the job than be fired.

All the kakistocrats receive compensation, benefits, pensions, and job security far greater than the average American. As our servants, we need to pay them fairly for their voluntary service, and that's it! Because we pay kakistocrats far more than the average Dutiful Cog, they work hard to stay for life in a system that provides great job security without judging the value of their performance. These kakistocrats need to be judged and compensated based on their adherence to the Constitution and the value they provide in return for our payments to them. We should do nothing to entice these kakistocrats to continue running our government as if it is their right. There should be no divine rights for kakistocrats!

Governance Principle 4

There Must Be Real Checks and Balances Between Branches of Government

For decades, the kakistocrats occupying the respective branches of government have been aligned by political party, not by branch of government. By doing so, they have created a system based on the power of political forces that ignores the separation of power required by the Constitution and the checks each branch must impose on the others. In the present system, we are a nation controlled by political organizations and collabortakers who have massive amounts of money, organization, and a need to possess power. These forces seek to render the individual and the Constitution of little import. This abuse, however, can be easily remedied by demanding that the kakistocrats be loyal to the institution in which they serve, not the political parties to which they belong or to the collabortakers who help them stay in power. This simple change will empower the respective institutions of government to serve as checks on the other branches. This simple change will greatly foster a more limited government that stays within its constitutionally stated responsibilities.

In our current system, all branches act to serve their political benefactors, collabortakers, and themselves. In addressing issues of political consequence the courts many times interpret our laws and the Constitution as if they were a legislature. The executive uses the bureaucracy to impose legislative mandates on all of us by issuing over two hundred thousand regulations. And, most troubling, through the passage of broad, vague laws, Congress, the sole legislative authority under the Constitution, delegates its powers to the executive so as to avoid the difficult decisions of making the laws and controlling the nation's finances. All decisions become about gaining and retaining power for the kakistocracy, not about checking the power of the respective branches of government.

To address this assault on the separation of powers required by the Constitution, every kakistocrat needs to publicly reaffirm their oath to support the Constitution and uphold the integrity and obligations of the institution in which they serve. Only by doing so will our institutions of government provide the checks we need on the political forces that seek only control over the people, their property, and the resources of the nation.

Governance Principle 5

The Executive and the Courts Must Voluntarily Limit Their Legislating Activities to Preserve the Constitution

The federal government was not always a massive, complex, bumbling bureaucracy. For most of our history, it was relatively small and limited. As a means of dealing with the Depression in the 1930s, the federal government enacted many laws to address social problems, ranging from labor relations to Social Security, banking regulations, and job creation. The growth of government did not stop after the Depression ended; it just continued, and its laws became even more complex in areas of economic and social regulation and wealth distribution. Each new law triggered many regulations, and most times court decisions upheld the regulatory expansion of the law by deferring to agency decisions. Now we have a multi-trillion-dollar-a-year federal government with hundreds of thousands of regulations that regulate almost every aspect of our existence, and a Congress that continues to enact more broad and vague laws that require even more regulations and constant court review, which results in greater expansion of the administrative state.

The result of the present process is continuously increasing government production of laws, regulations, guidance documents, enforcement activities, and judicial decisions that sweep across the nation, changing the ground rules in a way that few can understand. As the speed of change increases, it produces greater uncertainty as to how to deal with the kakistocracy, thereby impacting business investment, innovation, and even simple day-to-day activities.

Unfortunately, the kakistocracy under Democratic or Republican rule is always the same; it grows debt, complexity, and favor for the extremely well-off. All that is different are the names of the beneficiaries. The Democrat benefits environmentalist, unions, those who make money on government, and collabortakers. The Republican benefits hedge funds, banks, and corporations and collabortakers. In both administrations, the debt always grows and is placed on the balance sheets of the Dutiful Cogs for later payment while the collabortakers take the money and run. In the long term, our willingness to continually accept more debt being placed on future generations will gradually morph into a servile state, which uses the complexity of the system to exploit the Dutiful Cog for the payment of debt.

The only way to quickly control government is for each branch of government to voluntarily control the mandates it imposes on the nation. This could be accomplished with the use of common sense.

Congress would pass fewer and more rational laws if it merely worked in regular order by using committees, floor debates, conference committees, and open debates throughout. This, combined with oversight and funding only laws that are authorized, would allow Congress to read the laws it considers, provide proper oversight of the executive's implementation of the laws, and be better able to balance the competing needs within the country.

With fewer laws, the executive branch would issue fewer regulations, thus reducing its opportunities to act as the lawmaker. It is also more likely to more effectively implement congressional policy.

The judiciary, while being the interpreter of the Constitution, must grasp that it is not a legislature. To play its constitutional role, the judiciary, especially the lower courts, must avoid making sweeping pronouncements that create new laws, rights, or obligations. The judiciary must willingly restrain itself from legislating, and with Congress passing fewer laws and providing more oversight of agencies, it should have an easier task. If the judiciary cannot limit its tendency to legislate, Congress has the power under Articles I and III of the Constitution, to limit the jurisdiction of the inferior courts.

Our nation simply cannot be run by a group of unelected persons who believe that their role in the kakistocracy is that of a super-legislature. It is the role of Congress to ensure that the judiciary works within its constitutional and statutory limits and that Congress is the sole legislative branch.

Governance Principle 6

Laws Must Be Reduced and Simplified

Tacitus warned us that "the more corrupt the state, the more numerous its laws." The more numerous the laws, the larger the bureaucracy and the greater the complexity, resulting in the centralization of power in the hands of a few individuals, whose only goal is to hold power. The massive amount of power held by the kakistocracy is used solely as a weapon against us, not as a means of protecting our liberties or bettering our society.

The kakistocrats do not read or comprehend the laws they impose; they merely issue them to ensure that, at a time of their choosing, they can hold any one of us in violation. As more and more laws impose more complexity upon us, we have less understanding about how to act. With more laws and greater complexity, we become exhausted lawbreakers, lacking the will to challenge the kakistocracy, which is not open to change. The nation stagnates within its legal and bureaucratic complexity, to the point where all the kakistocracy can do is impose more laws to address every situation. Eventually, the legal and bureaucratic structure will collapse, and while the kakistocrats will lose their power, the nation, unfortunately, will live in chaos. Before chaos occurs, good governance requires the following:

1. Laws that are simple, clearly written, and capable of being understood by a person of average intelligence.
2. Every member of the legislative branch who votes on a law, every member of the executive branch who issues a regula-

tion, and every court that interprets a law or regulation to certify that they have read every word of the pronouncement and the background information that justifies the need for the law.

3. A substantial reduction in the thousands of laws enacted. By reducing the number of laws in effect, the kakistocracy automatically reduces the regulations needed to implement them.

4. Federal and state governments to negotiate and clearly allocate their respective management responsibilities and the allocation of costs.

5. Passing only those laws that the government is capable of paying for, implementing, and enforcing. By doing so, we will avoid laws just to have laws; otherwise, the common law should apply.

Governance Principle 7

The Functions of Government Must Be Performed at the Most Efficient Level of Government

No reasonable person would ever consciously design a legal and regulatory system as vast, complex, duplicative, and intrusive as the system we have in the United States, comprising hundreds of thousands of laws and regulations, the designation of thousands of actions as criminal, civil and administrative offenses—all enforced by a combination of federal, state, and local authorities. Since no person can fully understand our system of laws and regulations, it is unmanageable and arbitrary.

To humanize and foster respect for our system of laws and regulations, the functions of government must be performed at the most efficient level of government. We must restructure the government to clearly identify federal, state, and local responsibilities. Once the government's powers are distributed to the level most capable of administering allocated responsibilities, costs can be more equitably allocated, power will be limited, and citizens will be able to contact the level of government either responsible for the service to be provided or liable for the harm caused in the administration of the service. The moment this decentralizing force comes into existence, the kakistocracy will understand its responsibilities and the fiduciary nature of government service, the functions of government will become clearer to citizens, and those serving in government will become more responsible to citizens—or will be forced to leave the government. Services not managed by government that are needed by citizens will be more clearly identifiable, and citizens can better determine whether to assume the cost of a new government program or leave it to private enterprise to provide.

And while certain powers will remain with each level of government, each state will administer its laws differently, depending upon the will of the citizens, thus reflecting the personalities of the respective states, which will compete against each other for citizens, jobs, wealth, and quality of life.

Governance Principle 8

Government Must Focus on Priorities

No matter what the campaign promises or the good intentions of the kakistocrats, government cannot perform more services or provide more protections than can reasonably be performed with the resources made available to it by its citizens. Doing more without those resources can only be accomplished by mandates on citizens, the accumulation of which can result in tyranny; by theft, which results in poverty; or by complexity, which results in collapse. Although tyranny, theft, and collapse are the common attributes of the kakistocracy throughout history, it is not written that this must be our fate.

The kakistocracy must recognize that it is organized for a limited purpose: to protect its citizens from foreign invasion and the many from the violations of the few so that its citizens may pursue the common interest of achieving prosperity while being secure in their person. For in the final analysis, it is not government but the mutual and reciprocal interests between individuals that keep a society together. Government is merely organized to protect us from harm while we pursue our ends. As to laws, the more numerous they are, the more they become weapons of social destruction by picking winners and losers and pitting group against group. To restrain the kakistocracy from its natural tendency of tyranny, theft, and eventual collapse, we citizens must work to ensure that the functions of government can never extend beyond those powers necessary to protect us, our property, and our liberty. Responsible governance requires the following:

1. The federal government must prioritize its actions by addressing first the most important governmental responsibilities, for example, national defense, protecting citizens from harm, and protecting private property.

2. The respective states must use their constitutionally established police powers to ensure our basic protections from the few who would violate us and deprive us of our rights. Moreover, the state, as the primary government of general authority, should provide whatever programs it can with the monies paid to it by the people. Each state will have a different relationship with its citizens. Some states and their citizens will want more open participation in the private market, whereas others will be willing to pay for more government services. Those decisions should be made by the citizens of the respective states.

3. The federal courts must hear and rule only upon controversies between the parties before the court and within the limited jurisdiction of the court, while state courts hear general state and common-law claims.

4. Private associations, to the extent of the trust placed in them by the citizens, should, to the maximum extent practicable, manage and regulate general business practices in lieu of government, and such associations and their members will be responsible for enforcement of their standards and liable for harm caused by any breach of duty.

5. The activities of society must be managed more by contract than regulation with liability attaching to any breach, negligent performance, or intentional harm. Contracts are a quicker and easier mechanism to enforce than attempting to persuade the kakistocracy to act in addressing every wrong.

Governance Principle 9

Government Must Be More Than Transparent—It Must Be Understandable

"Transparency" is a word regularly uttered by kakistocrats that sounds full of truth and openness, but it is used to promote deception. With an unquantifiable number of secret meetings, massive numbers of documents, endless statistics, computer models, and scientific studies, countless experts, a vast number of spies, and the largest military in the world, complete transparency is impossible for the kakistocracy. It can, however, provide sufficient relevant information so that citizens can assess whether their government is taking action consistent with or adverse to the fiduciary relationship to its citizens. For citizens to make informed decisions, the kakistocracy needs to provide us with information that:

1. clearly and accurately discloses the overall impact of a law or regulation on present and future generations, who will receive proceeds or benefits from the kakistocracy, as well as environmental, social, and economic impacts, including indirect impacts;
2. provides all information that it relies upon in decision-making, including the computer models used, all assumptions made, and a list of all persons who sought to influence the decisions;

3. discloses all monies expended to influence its decisions, and the persons making the expenditures must immediately record them for the public to review;

4. discloses all monies paid by any third-party organization to another to influence the decision-making of the kakistocracy;

5. immediately discloses all persons meeting with kakistocrats and the subject matter of the meetings, and any requests made of kakistocrats and by kakistocrats with those in the meetings;

6. informs the public with thirty days' notice of all grants it gives to anyone, and all contracts it enters into with anyone;

7. makes available kakistocrats' calendars at the beginning of every day;

8. immediately discloses all monies and items of value received by a kakistocrat while serving the nation;

9. identifies all lawsuits filed against it and provides thirty days' notice of any potential settlements of the lawsuits involving public policy; and

10. provides a monthly accounting of all receipts and expenditures of public monies, including the names of all recipients.

Governance Principle 10

Government Must Operate Only for the Public Purpose

The kakistocracy operates under the golden rule: "He who has the gold rules." Any restraints on the golden rule, such as the meaning and intent of the General Welfare Clause of the Constitution, have been debated since the beginning of the republic, only to conclude that the kakistocrat with the power generally determines the meaning of the Constitution, acts of Congress, and regulations. So, debating whether there are limits to the power of the kakistocracy is a futile effort. There are very few limits on the kakistocracy to spend our money, pass new laws, regulate, or broaden the scope of a law by judicial fiat.

The real question is, how do we create a balance in the kakistocracy to promote spending that truly builds the nation while preventing the direct redistribution of wealth to strictly private enterprises that wield influence in the kakistocracy? While the legal answer is that the kakistocracy holds the power to interpret and enforce the law, the practical answer is that unless we demand that any wealth redistribution be limited to truly public purposes, the kakistocracy will continue to reward its friends while bankrupting the nation. To ensure that our money is spent to achieve a public purpose, the kakistocracy needs to follow some basic rules:

1. Other than Social Security, Medicare and Medicaid, which are discussed in Part IV: Restructuring the Automatic

Withdrawals of Taxpayers Assets, appropriations can only be used to promote a purpose that benefits the public-at-large. All grants, low-interest loans, subsidies, and tax credits to private entities would be prohibited.

2. Congress must limit its power to tax to amounts needed to support priority functions of the federal government; other general taxes will rest with states and local governments that are much closer and responsible to the people.

3. As the kakistocracy operates more as a fiduciary to guard public assets, there will be less government procurement, which will result in smaller government. Less government will result in less of our wealth in the hands of kakistocrats to redistribute to their friends.

4. By having a smaller federal government that has less money for redistribution, two important realities will occur. First, the kakistocracy will be smaller, with power more distributed throughout the nation, and this will serve as a real check on the kakistocracy. Second, the true interests of the nation will become paramount as the funds available in the Treasury for private gain are reduced. When this occurs, the kakistocrats will focus on the true interests of the nation, making us better, more just, and more competitive.

Part III

A Few Modest Proposals for Restructuring the Kakistocracy

The Kakistocracy's Breach of Its Fiduciary Duty Necessitates Its Restructuring

Since the time of Plato, the citizens of a republic have believed that a government is formed when individuals consent to surrender some of their freedoms to the government in exchange for protection of their remaining rights. Certainly, these beliefs have evolved over time as societies, science, and technologies have changed. But what has never changed is the belief that for citizens in a democracy, there is a direct relationship, be it fiduciary duty or contract, between those who are governed and those who govern that defines the rights of the people and the responsibilities of the government. Underlying this theory is the belief that the state exists only to serve the people, who are the source of all political power. In the case of the United States, it is the Constitution that clearly defines the limits of the powers exercised by the federal government.

When the powers of the federal government exceed the powers given to it by our Constitution, there is a breach of fiduciary duty by the government to its citizens. This breach has occurred as the federal government has morphed into a kakistocracy by accumulating massive amounts of power over every aspect of our lives, and by converting the states of the union into servants that administer federal programs. If this breach of duty is not soon remedied, the governing entity that has become a kakistocracy will soon control all of our society. As this occurs, our rights will be gradually lost to the kakistocracy. The final result will be citizens answering to the demands of the kakistocracy. The kakistocracy will be our master, and we will be its servants.

The divergence between us and the kakistocracy is easily illustrated. To maintain control over us, kakistocrats promise benefits they know they cannot deliver. As we continue accepting whatever promises they make to us, we are making the involuntary servitude of future generations more certain.

The kakistocracy preaches free markets in which we can all fairly compete for the fruits generated by society, but it structures laws so that only kakistocrats and collabortakers can prevail. These same kakistocrats and collabortakers justify the massive benefits they take from society by branding themselves as "irreplaceable job creators," yet our wages are stagnant, and jobs and industries have been relocating to foreign countries for decades.

Kakistocrats and collabortakers argue that we need to control payments to the elderly, the poor, and the disabled because they are increasing at such a massive rate the country will be bankrupt, yet according to Professor Emmanuel Saez, since 2009 approximately ninety percent of all income gains in our nation have gone to the top one percent of the income earners. The kakistocrats are willing to provide hundreds of billions in subsidies to the collabortakers, who caused the financial collapse of the nation in the first decade of the twenty-first century, but constantly harp on the rising cost of the financial safety net for the needy. Moreover, these same collabortakers have lawyers and accountants secure low tax rates and trust arrangements that allow them to shelter income for generations while the taxes paid by labor cannot be shifted, and they personally benefit from hundreds of billions of dollars in government grants, loans, and contracts.

The kakistocracy has breached its duty to act in a manner that binds the nation together. This is not a battle of rich versus poor or jealousy of another's riches; it is merely a recognition that the kakistocrats and collabortakers, by controlling our government, manipulating the legal system, and managing corporations for their benefit, have taken the gains created by the work of the Dutiful Cogs and left them with massive debt, a legal and tax system so complicated it cannot be understood, and a dim future for our children. These breaches of duty have been inflicted upon us by an arrogant group of people who believe they are entitled to manage our government for their personal benefit. And yes, while the nation must address the social entitlements given to the needy that we truly cannot afford, the nation must also address massive wealth transfer to the kakisto-crats and collabortakers, which we also cannot afford.

To address these breaches, the citizens of this nation must restructure their relationship with the kakistocracy to ensure every kakistocrat fulfills their fiduciary duty to us.

Restructuring Proposal 1

Congress Must Reclaim Its Role as the Primary Legislative Body

Nothing in our Constitution could be clearer in intent and meaning than the first sentence, which reads: "All legislative Powers herein granted shall be vested in a Congress of the United States, which shall consist of a Senate and House of Representatives."

To fulfill this constitutional mandate, Congress needs to act as an institution that both legislates and checks the powers of the executive and the courts when those institutions legislate through overreaching regulation or sweeping judicial opinions.

We Dutiful Cogs must replace the members of Congress who demonstrate greater loyalty to their political party than to the Constitution by electing individuals who are loyal to the institution of Congress and willing to provide the checks on the other branches to ensure that Congress is the prime lawmaker. When the members of Congress become more loyal to the political parties they are members of than the Congress they are elected to, Congress morphs from a constitutional bulwark into a political association. Even more insidious is when members of Congress and the executive are of the same party. These members generally give all loyalty to the executive, thus abdicating their primary role as a check on the powers of the other branches of government.

Notwithstanding the declarative constitutional statement on the powers of Congress, we find ourselves living in an age where Congress has lost its legislative powers to the federal administrative state, which determines what Congress intends and legislates through regulation to put its policies into effect. Compounding this travesty, the federal courts provide great deference to the decisions of the administrative state by upholding its regulations. Moreover, the courts, on more than a few occasions, legislate by issuing orders that expand laws in ways never intended by Congress. These actions place Congress in a state of helplessness, unless it can muster a supermajority of its members to overrule the executive and the courts, an almost impossible task.

Once in this state of helplessness, Congress has only one power to control the administrative state: the power of the purse. Under our Constitution, "No Money shall be drawn from the Treasury, but in Consequence of Appropriations made by Law." If the party that's not the executive's party controls even one house of Congress, it can withhold the monies needed to run the parts of the administrative state it believes are acting improperly or are unnecessary. While withholding the funds to operate the administrative state is viewed by many as abhorrent, it is the only constitutional power left to Congress that cannot be blocked by the other branches. If the power of appropriations cannot be used out of fear of political backlash, then it is a useless power for controlling the administrative state, ensuring the administrative state's control of our government, our resources, and all citizens.

To address this failure, we citizens must demand that every member of Congress pledge to support and defend the institution of Congress and its powers to legislate and appropriate funds and to act as a check on the other branches of government as intended by our Constitution. If a person seeking election to Congress cannot make and keep this pledge, we must withhold our vote from that person, which is the only real power to control the kakistocracy.

Restructuring Proposal 2

Restructuring of the Kakistocracy Must Include Everything the Kakistocrats Manage

Complex societies collapse. Massively indebted societies collapse. Societies with their militaries deployed throughout the world collapse. Highly regulated societies collapse. We are all these combined, and the kakistocrats contentedly sit in a bubble, unable to address any of the serious risks confronting our nation. They completely delude themselves that collapse can't happen here. It has happened to every major empire in the history of the world, and it will happen here unless the risks are addressed. And as with all collapses, our society will live with the risk perhaps for decades, but then some sudden event will initiate a collapse, and the kakistocrats will be helpless to address it. At that point, the entire society will go into the abyss. Once in the abyss, it can take centuries to reemerge from the darkness as chaos rules.

There are times in the history of nations when the citizens need to act before those entrusted with the control and resources of the nation cause it harm. Now is the time for action! Citizens must immediately demand that the kakistocrats act as fiduciaries and address the risks to our nation. If the kakistocrats refuse or ignore their responsibility to manage the risks confronting the nation, they need to resign their offices and let others with more courage assume the task as fiduciaries of the nation.

What would be sufficient structural reform? Everything must be considered: taxes, spending, selling of assets, elimination of overreaching laws and regulations, and transfer to the states the laws and powers they can implement better than the federal government. This process must start with the federal government and the states negotiating what is the most efficient distribution of power for the management of a complex society. As a nation, we may want to avoid these difficult issues, but if we do, we must always remember that empires collapse and governments default on debt they have incurred to maintain their power. There is never a right time to take on difficult issues; there is only now.

Restructuring Proposal 3

The Kakistocracy Must Devolve Power to the States

The kakistocracy has legislated to itself, via the federal government, massive amounts of power over the entire society. Without having the means to pay for the massive structure it has created, it commandeers the states through promises of federal payments for implementing its complex and costly programs, many of which the federal government should not be running, such as education, energy, health care, agriculture, and hundreds of minor programs.

To address this power grab by the kakistocracy, the federal government and the states should negotiate which programs would be best managed by each and transfer those best managed by the states to the states. Such a negotiation will be extremely difficult. The kakistocrats and the collabortakers passionately want to continue accumulating power, and they will initially refuse to cede any power to the states, which they view as mere servants of the kakistocracy.

The state legislatures, however, do have leverage; it is only a question of whether some or all the states will use it. But if enough states use their leverage, the kakistocracy will concede. First, all states administer many federal programs and are reimbursed only a fraction of the cost of administration. The states could merely return all these programs to the federal government. Such a brazen act will initially cause chaos as the federal government would be unable to administer these programs. As a power play, the kakistocracy would likely retaliate by refusing to issue federal permits for facilities operating in noncooperating states. States would have to sue the federal government, thus allowing the courts to determine the allocation of responsibilities between the federal and state governments.

While the legal process slowly works its way through the courts, there would be chaos in the states, but the states' actions would clearly demonstrate to the federal government their essential role in our system of federalism. It would also demonstrate that the federal government, without state cooperation, cannot manage or pay for the government it has created. During the chaos the kakistocracy would need to negotiate with the states just to maintain a figment of power or watch federal programs collapse without the money or staff to implement them. This puts the states at the negotiating table with the federal government. At this point the serious negotiations over the allocation of powers and responsibilities begin.

An alternative approach would be for the states to utilize Article V of the Constitution, which requires Congress, upon "the application of the Legislatures of two thirds of the several States...[to] call a Convention for proposing Amendments, which...shall be valid to all Intents and Purposes, as Part of this Constitution, when ratified by the Legislatures of three fourths of the several States, or by Conventions in three fourths thereof."

An objective of the convention would be for the states to clearly set forth the scope of federal authority. The kakistocracy would never allow a threat of this magnitude to materialize. Before the states ever acquired the needed consent, the kakistocracy, through Congress, would initiate its own Article V convention so it could limit the scope of the state-called convention. Or perhaps it would voluntarily begin devolving power to the states to blunt the state effort for a convention.

The states can no longer ignore having their sovereignty diminished by the kakistocracy. The states need to assume their rightful role as sovereigns that share power with the federal government for the sake of their citizens, for posterity, and for the Constitution. The kakistocracy needs to recognize that it has amassed such great amounts of power that it cannot manage the powers it has taken.

While neither action by the states is likely to intimidate the kakistocracy into relinquishing the powers it has taken from the states and their citizens, both actions are legal mechanisms to start a constitutional revolution to limit the massive size and coercive nature of the kakistocracy. Both actions clearly illustrate that the kakistocracy is unable to manage our government without the help of the states and their citizens. Once this is recognized, it should make it easier for the kakistocracy to begin devolving power to those best able to exercise it.

Restructuring Proposal 4

Congress Must Reestablish the Joint Committee on the Reduction of Nonessential Federal Expenditures

When Congress passes a law, the new law mandates that regulations be written. As Congress passes more and more laws, it mandates that bureaucrats issue more and more regulations. Congress has placed enormous power in the control of the kakistocrats who occupy the agencies that determine what these laws mean. This process transfers the legislative power from Congress to the bureaucracy. This transfer of power is so direct that if regulations are not written, private parties can bring a lawsuit to mandate the regulation be issued. Therefore, it is simple: if Congress truly wants to reduce the hundreds of thousands of regulations imposed on the citizens of the nation, it must reduce the number of laws in effect.

During World War II, massive defense expenditures dramatically expanded the nation's debt, and for a few years, our debt exceeded the nation's GDP. Today we are again experiencing a dramatically expanded debt, which now stands at approximately ninety percent of the GDP. The distinguishing factor between our debt in the 1940s and today is that the 1940s Congress knew the debt needed to be reduced and took action. It established the Joint Committee on Reduction of Nonessential Federal Expenditures, led by Senator Harry Byrd of Virginia. While not a legislative committee, its goal was to identify nonessential federal expenditures and government agencies and make recommendations for eliminating or reducing them. Many of the committee's recommendations were acted upon by the legislative committees of Congress and enacted into law, such as the elimination of several New Deal programs.

If Congress is to reduce the federal deficit and regulations, it must create a new Joint Committee on Reduction of Nonessential Federal Expenditures to examine the need for and benefits from the tens of thousands of laws that are in effect and to recommend which laws and agencies the nation can do without. Moreover, as part of its devolution efforts, Congress could also identify the federal laws that could be more effectively and efficiently managed by the states and provide recommendations on devolving responsibility for those to the states. Only by reducing unneeded laws and transferring to the states federal functions more appropriate for state action can the nation begin to reduce its deficit and the regulations imposed on the American people.

Restructuring Proposal 5

Spending Must Be Limited to Essential Activities

As the kakistocracy devolves the management of certain activities to the states, and the activities of government are at the most efficient level for managing those activities, there will be fewer federal laws and regulations. With less federal activity, there will be a need for fewer kakistocrats and less spending on the operations of the federal government. This is a very positive start in controlling spending and the massive size of the federal government. But far more is required if citizens are to gain management control over the kakistocracy.

Concurrent with devolution of powers to the states, Congress should order an audit of every remaining federal program (other than Social Security, Medicare, and Medicaid, which are discussed in Part IV: Restructuring the Automatic Withdrawals of Taxpayers Assets) to determine its costs, beneficiaries, effectiveness in achieving its goals, and value intended by Congress. With this information, the kakistocrats must then rank every program in order of need, value, and efficiency. The highest-priority programs will be funded first. The kakistocrats would work down the list of priorities until the revenue raised by taxes is expended. At that point, Congress would have to cease spending money on programs for which there is no longer any funding. Also, by designating programs as low value, Congress would be foolish to authorize additional borrowing for them.

Setting priorities will be a difficult task as the kakistocrats, and especially the collabortakers, like spending our money for their purposes without limit. Until we require the kakistocrats to audit and prioritize every program, we cannot complete the restructuring of our government. The kakistocrats will strongly resist prioritizing federal programs, but as more individuals who are willing to serve as fiduciaries are elected to Congress, the kakistocrats will come to realize that their very existence depends on being honest with the American people and serving as fiduciaries of the nation.

Restructuring Proposal 6

Congress Must Not Appropriate
Money for Unauthorized Laws

The laws passed by Congress generally fall into two groups:

a. Those authorized for a set period of time, for example, three or five years, and that need appropriations by Congress to pay for their implementation. These laws are referred to as discretionary spending laws. Appropriations are needed to implement these laws. At the end of each congressionally authorized period, they need to be reauthorized.

b. Those that have no expiration date and for which Congress mandates continuous funding, for example, Social Security. These are referred to as mandatory spending laws or entitlements.

Understanding this distinction is important in efforts to reduce laws and regulations. Simply, as the authorization period of a discretionary law expires, Congress has the opportunity to review it, reauthorize it, amend it, or allow it to lapse. Just using the reauthorization process gives Congress the ability to regain control over parts of the legislative process and, by extension, the regulatory process, as fewer laws means fewer regulations. This point can be clearly illustrated.

For many years, Congress has been generally unable to establish a budget or pass all its appropriations bills. Usually, Congress just bundles hundreds of billions of dollars into a Continuing Resolution or omnibus appropriation to fund disparate laws and programs, with little understanding of where the monies will be spent. Congress does this bundling to keep the government functioning and avoid public criticism for letting it shut down. In this mindless process, however, Congress performs one act that debases the institution and provides perpetual power to the growth of the bureaucracy. This mindless act is a parliamentary procedure, the deeming of unauthorized laws to be authorized for purposes of making appropriations, that gives life to all those laws that have expired and that Congress fails to review.

Congress could simply not reauthorize laws with lapsed authorization, but it does not. Call it hypocrisy, fear, ignorance, politics, or whatever—in the end, Congress avoids taking control of the legislative process by merely deeming laws reauthorized, notwithstanding the fact that it does not conduct oversight of those laws or reauthorize them through the formal legislative process of hearings, committee votes, floor votes, and conference committees.

Such legislating, however, is contrary to almost two centuries of legislative practice for funding the implementation of laws. While there was always an informal process that required that Congress first pass a substantive law and then appropriate monies to implement the law, Congress formalized this process as early as 1837, when the House of Representatives provided by rule that "no appropriation shall be reported in such general appropriations bills, or be in order as an amendment thereto, for any expenditure not previously authorized by law."

This prohibition continues today for appropriations voted as part of regular order, but it does not apply to the continuing resolutions that have become a mainstay of modern legislating. As such, Congress appropriates monies to implement laws that have expired merely by deeming them authorized or funding them through a Continuing Resolution.

Under the rules of the House of Representatives, a legislator can raise a point of order against appropriations for laws not authorized by statute. Once raised, the point of order is debated. Unfortunately, as a means of avoiding responsibility for not examining laws at the time of their expiration, Congress allows the point of order to be overturned by a majority vote, notwithstanding that the majority vote conflicts with its policy that a law must be authorized before appropriations can be made for its implementation. Congress also allows itself by rule to waive the point of order, again allowing a practice that circumvents its own rules.

By circumventing its own rules, Congress avoids having to make the difficult decisions on which laws should continue to be in effect. It merely allows all laws to remain in effect. Though this charade may be an easy way for Congress to avoid doing its job, it is a prime reason why it cannot control the growth of laws and regulations. In hundreds of instances, Congress has funded laws that were not reauthorized in years—in some instances, decades. According to the Congressional Budget Office, Congress appropriated tens of billions of dollars to fund hundreds of laws with expired authorizations. The unauthorized laws being funded by Congress are found throughout all activities of the federal government, from the environment to the Departments of Justice, Energy, Commerce, and Housing. By undertaking this practice of deeming unauthorized laws authorized so appropriations can be made to implement them, Congress has put the growth of the bureaucracy on autopilot.

Congress cannot continue to appropriate our money for a bureaucracy to implement laws that it fails to reauthorize. Congress must bring fiscal and regulatory sanity to government. Congress does not need to shut down the entire government; all it needs is for a few brave members to stand up and force a vote to deny funding to specific programs that it has not reauthorized. Members of Congress have a choice to review each law and reauthorize, amend, or terminate it, or to publicly waive the rules for expediency. Of course, congressional leadership will likely push hard to deem all those unauthorized programs technically authorized, but at that point, it will be obvious which of the elected kakistocrats simply refuse to be responsible for their legislative duties.

As more and more members raise points of order to stop the funding of expired laws, Congress, for the first time in decades, will begin examining each law that requires reauthorization. This process will force Congress into understanding what it has enacted and how these laws impact the American people. As this process moves forward, Congress will reduce its budget deficits by tens of billions annually, simply by pruning laws that do not achieve their purpose, or for which the costs greatly outweigh the benefits. Just reviewing the laws in need of reauthorization begins to put Congress back in control of the legislative process and the growth of regulations and bureaucracy. By having this process unfold law by law, Congress will not be in the uncomfortable situation of shutting down the government for lack of funding; rather, it will only defund laws it has not found worthy of reauthorization or for which there is great dispute as to need and effectiveness. Simply, Congress needs to play by the rules it established. It needs to stop deeming as authorized laws that have not been reauthorized, and it must start reauthorizing needed laws and letting the less useful laws lapse.

Restructuring Proposal 7

Regulatory Complexity Must Be Reversed

The direct result of devolving power to the level of government that can manage the issue more efficiently is that there will be far less government, as the current system encourages the regulation of the same activity by federal, state, and, at times, local government. By having only one layer of government administering specific activities, there will simply be fewer laws administered at each level. This will be one of the few times in modern history that a nation will reduce its number of laws. Moreover, it is only by eliminating laws that we can eliminate regulations.

Fewer laws will lessen government interference in citizens' lives. With less need to regulate, government should be creative in developing a new and more efficient regulatory process for the laws it administers. Less emphasis should be placed on a command-and-control government process that mandates every detail of a regulatory system. The nation needs a new theory of how to regulate, one that achieves the same level of health, safety, and consumer protection but at far lower cost and with less intrusion. There are many alternatives that would achieve this objective.

Presently, private entities, such as standard-setting organizations, establish industry best practices and product standards that align industry promises, warranties, risks, and liabilities in a way that ensures that the industry has a collective interest in safe products and performance. These best practices provide operational and safety standards, training, and certification programs backed by sufficient insurance protection, all paid for by the sector establishing the standards. Enforcement can be maintained through contract, insurance and insurance audits, product evaluation, arbitration, or civil and criminal liability for violations of the standards or anti-competitive conduct, or through the imposition of enterprise liability, a theory where the industry setting the standards remains liable for not ensuring compliance. Though the process is voluntary, it is a promise to the public that can be enforced through a variety of mechanisms. The industries that make the promise can advertise it, and government and the public have the means to enforce it. Those entities that do not participate in the standard setting process would have to inform the public that they are not complying with the standards and therefore are not legally able to make any representations about the quality or safety of their product. For companies that fail to adopt industry standards, it is truly a "buyer beware" situation.

Under this self-regulatory standard-setting process, the government acts as the umpire to ensure that the public is protected, while always being able to stop abuse. Such a system will be less costly, provide equal or greater protection of health and safety, and be easier to implement, since industries, using the best experts in the world, will develop standards that make their operations safer than anything the government could devise.

Moreover, because liability for harm rests on the industry that develops and implements the standards, it will impose the most protective of standards to avoid as much liability as possible. In addition, the insurers, as a means of protecting themselves, will continuously conduct operational audits of companies to ensure compliance with best practices. Under this privately developed regulatory system, there will be greater innovation to foster even better and safer operations, as a private entity can develop new standards that incorporate the newest technologies at a much faster pace than a government agency. The public will be better protected, and the government, without having to develop every operational detail, will have more time and resources to perform oversight to ensure compliance by businesses, insurers, and auditors. At all times, responsibility for breach or harm would remain with the entity and/or industry offering the product or service, or its insurance and audit providers.

Another alternative to the current command-and-control regulatory process is for the government to set performance standards and for businesses to have the discretion to meet the standards in the most cost-efficient manner. To monitor compliance, government could require regular compliance audits and adequate insurance and exercise emergency powers in times of major accidents or violations. Again, without government involvement in every step of the regulatory process, businesses have flexibility, and government can more efficiently ensure compliance.

Principle-based regulation is another way to regulate. Government would set broad principles, and the regulated community would determine how best to achieve them. The role of government would be to audit the compliance of the regulated community and take civil or criminal action against violators. Although principle-based regulation is more uncertain than command-and-control regulation, it has many benefits. Specifically, the regulated community can usually maneuver around the language in a specific regulation and avoid penalty. In a principle-based system, the goal is to ensure that the regulated entity achieves the goals of the principle, for example, protect health, safety, and consumers, not just the details of a regulation. The downside of the principle-based regulatory process is that many of the decisions defining the standards are determined by the courts, but the process has worked well for centuries under the common law.

Finally, even if the kakistocracy insists on a command-and-control regulatory system, one way to bring greater certainty of implementation is to require that all regulations once issued remain unchanged for at least ten years, except for emergency matters. This would dramatically lessen the regulatory churn of routinely revising regulations and provide certainty for the regulated community.

There is no perfect regulatory process, but there are alternatives that should be utilized to ensure that the details of the process do not overwhelm the activities of the market. Presently in the United States, the command-and-control regulatory process is the primary system. It is costly, complex, time-consuming, and over-bearing. To alleviate regulatory overreach, the remaining agencies need to consider all regulatory options and align their objectives with the option that is the most cost-efficient for achieving congressional intent.

Restructuring Proposal 8

The Kakistocracy Must Sell
All Unnecessary Assets

The federal government has buildings and massive landholdings throughout the world. Some of its holdings are critical to its mission; some are critical to the United States, such as great national parks; some are critical to food, mineral, or energy production and provide the federal government with significant royalties. But many of its property holdings are surplus properties, abandoned or partially occupied buildings, parks that the government neglects to maintain, and disparate parcels of land that could be sold for development without any adverse impact on any aspect of government operations. The revenues from the sale of these assets should be applied to reducing the debt.

Immediately, an inventory of federal properties and their use and status should be prepared. All properties and buildings that are needed to operate the government or have recreational, cultural, or historic significance should be retained. For example, the top sixty percent of properties on the priority list should be retained, and all other properties should be sold or returned to the respective states. All unoccupied or partially occupied buildings and disparate and scattered properties that have no current operational use or are not being maintained should be sold. While not trillions of dollars in value, it would bring in billions of dollars. This is not only a necessary down payment on reducing the debt, it also takes a great amount of liability off the federal government's balance sheet by reducing management time, maintenance, and risk. Unfortunately, the federal government does not understand that the more property and infrastructure it owns, the costlier it is to manage and maintain. The federal government must keep important and needed property, but it must also sell unneeded and low-priority property to reduce the debt and operating expenses.

Restructuring Proposal 9

The Western Lands Must Be
Returned to the States

Other than defense installations and high priority National Parks and Monuments, the kakistocracy needs to return control of the western lands to the states that ceded the lands to the federal government as the price of admission to the union. As an owner of these western lands, the federal government has placed restrictions on grazing fees, timber harvesting, mining, and oil and gas reserves, imposing severe limits not only on wealth creation in the West but also citizens' ability to populate those lands, thereby limiting the political importance of the West in the union. Limiting the political influence of the western states started at the Constitutional Convention, when Governor Morris and Delegate Gerry forcefully argued for limited representation from the West, because if such "unenlightened people" obtained power, they would ruin the interests of the Atlantic states.

While such blatant discrimination of the soon-to-be western territories was voted down, the Convention did authorize Congress to make all rules and regulations respecting the western territory or other property belonging to the United States. Using this rule-making power, Congress admitted the western states into the union on the same footing with the original states. However, from the start, Congress discriminated against the western states by requiring them to disclaim all right and title to unappropriated lands lying within their boundaries. Unlike the Atlantic states, very little of the land of the territories was appropriated by private parties, allowing the early kakistocrats to grab up to eighty percent of all the land in the western states, depending on the state.

The tension between the western states and the kakistocracy in Washington is no less today than at the time of the western states' admission to the union. Some ranchers have threatened to block the kakistocrats' access to the land by force. Others have filed lawsuits, arguing that the federal government does not have a deed to the property, or that federal ownership of such vast amounts of land denies the various western states admission to the union on equal footing with the other states. The resentment stems from the simple fact that by forcing the cession of such large amounts of land to the federal government, the western states, unlike the Atlantic states, lost control of hundreds of millions of acres of land. This perpetually limited their population, their representation in Congress, and their ability to develop their economy and compete in the world.

By perpetually being disadvantaged by having limited representation in Congress, the western states can never be on an equal footing with the other states. Moreover, the kakistocracy does not have the money or competency to manage the land. The kakistocracy manages the land as an absentee landlord with little concern for the property or its inhabitants. More frustrating to the western states is that they have no recourse against their own federal government, which demanded the land and now abandons its care. And without the ability to grow its population due to the federal ownership of its land, the West has limits on increasing its political power in Congress.

The western lands need to be returned to the states, not only because they are within the borders of the respective states, and the states would better care for the land, but also because the federal government breached its promise to admit the western states into the union on an equal footing with the other states.

Restructuring Proposal 10

Congress Should Not Give Taxpayer Money to Private Entities

Congress should not give taxpayers money to private entities. Since the beginning of the republic, there has been a debate over whether Congress can spend our money only on what is specifically enumerated in the Constitution or is free to spend it on anything it believes to be in the general welfare. Continuing to debate this issue is irrelevant; the courts have made it clear that Congress determines what is the general welfare and that almost all appropriations are for a public purpose. Such a broad interpretation of Congress's ability to tax and spend has resulted in a massive increase in the national debt, a huge expansion of government, and countless numbers of grants to special interests, special projects, and special friends, ranging from infrastructure projects to bailouts of banks and automobile companies to funding of unworkable energy projects.

While there is almost no limit to the granting of such gifts by the kakistocrats in Congress, there are historical precedents for limiting such gifts to private entities. In the mid-1800s, many municipalities and states used public funds to purchase stock in the railroads being built across the continent. Many of these government entities lost or were swindled out of large amounts of taxpayer money. To prevent this type of financial loss in the future, forty-seven states enacted constitutional limitations preventing gifts to private entities. These limits placed on public spending came to be called "gift clauses."

The general gift clause prohibited state and local governments from giving or loaning public funds to private corporations or associations, or for private undertakings. The sole purpose of these gift clauses was to prohibit the gifting of public money for nonpublic purposes. Initially, these provisions stopped government speculation with taxpayer money and the gifting of public money to private entities. Over time, however, the courts began to legislate exceptions to the prohibitions for what they construed as a "public purpose"; for example, public funds could be given to a private entity if the gift would somehow result in a public benefit. The courts expanded the definition of "public benefit" to include almost anything the legislature thought was a public benefit. Such gifts now can be seen in almost every type of government project, from parking lots to sports facilities to corporate rent subsidies, to outright gifts to attract business to a state or locality, to grants and credits to incentivize politically favored forms of energy. Taxpayer money just flows, and the courts find it legal, since the appropriations carry the proof that the legislature intended them for a public purpose.

The mere fact that the public purpose exceptions have been grafted onto the gift clause by the courts is a prime example of courts acting as legislative bodies. We know that the kakistocrats on the courts, like those in Congress and in the executive branch, will do whatever they need to spend our money on their friends and allies. But stating that kakistocrats make gifts to friends is like stating that we need water to live. The important aspect of the issue is that we the people need to demand the enactment of a federal gift clause to limit how the kakistocracy spends our money. And while no one believes that the kakistocrats in Congress will ever enact a gift clause, each of us needs to demand every person running for Congress to take the following pledge:

> I pledge that, as a member of Congress, I will not vote to give, grant, or loan public funds or to extend the credit of the public to any private corporation, association, or private undertaking, and neither shall I vote to allow public

funds to be used for the purpose of taking stock
or investing in private corporations or any other
private undertaking.

By asking every person who seeks election to Congress to take
this pledge, citizens will easily distinguish between kakistocrats and
people seeking to protect the public monies we send to the government. Even after the election, if the pledge is broken, the public will
know who is trustworthy and who is not. The entire effort becomes
self-policing by citizens.

Restructuring Proposal 11

It Must Not Be Financially Attractive to Stay in the Kakistocracy

Every day, most citizens toil for every dollar they earn, while the kakistocrats we hire to manage the government and regulate us receive wages and retirement benefits substantially greater than most citizens can earn. Additionally, they receive all holidays off with pay, a handsome vacation package, the ability to work flexible hours, training of choice, regular in-step salary increases notwithstanding performance, incentive awards, and a bonus—and, most important, it is almost impossible to fire these kakistocrats for anything other than gross misconduct. As performance is never a question, and accountability is unknown, it is no wonder these kakistocrats who regulate us have a better chance of dying on the job than looking for a job in the private sector.

What do these kakistocrats do for us that is deserving of such largesse? As the list of missteps in the introduction identifies, they have created a society that is so complex it cannot be understood by persons of average intelligence; squandered the assets of countless government programs; given contracts, tax benefits, and grants to friends without concern for the public; and mismanaged government programs to the point that out of the tens of thousands of them, it is unlikely that the average American could identify even a handful that are workable.

In short, the kakistocrats who regulate us are provided a lifetime of security while we work every day to pay the bills. The kakistocrats have established themselves as a permanent upper class that is guaranteed benefits, no matter how poor their performance or how lacking in results and achievement. Under the present legal structure, these kakistocrats have laws that protect them from the American people. But as we reduce the federal government through devolution of power to the most efficient level, the ranks of the kakistocrats will have to shrink.

Unfortunately, devolution takes time, but as it is occurring, there may be a few actions Congress could take to urge these lavishly compensated kakistocrats to relinquish control over us Americans. First, Congress could let their pay and benefits remain at the same level as today until such time as the level equals that paid for similar jobs in the private sector. Second, all kakistocrats in the bureaucracy should be subject to term limits, under the principle that bureaucrats should not have the ability to hold power over Americans for their entire lives. No person should have that power. To ensure that the kakistocracy is restructured, Congress must limit the time in office for kakistocrats who regulate us to twelve years.

Restructuring Proposal 12

States Need to Assume Their Constitutional Role in Governing the Nation

If Congress refuses to negotiate the devolution of some significant powers to the states and remains unable to secure its role as our nation's primary legislative body, then the respective states must exercise their constitutional responsibilities under Article V of the Constitution.

Article V provides that Congress:

> ...on the application of the legislatures of two-thirds of the several states, shall call a Convention for proposing Amendments to the Constitution. Such Amendments shall be valid for all intents and purposes, as part of the Constitution, when ratified by the Legislatures of three-fourths of the several states or by a Convention in three-fourths thereof, as the one or the other Mode of Ratification may be proposed by the Congress.

While the Article V amending procedure has never been utilized, it is the only constitutional safety valve that allows the citizens of the nation, working through their state legislatures, to make changes to the Constitution without the approval of Congress, the president, or even the governors of the respective states. It simply allows the people working through their elected state legislatures to regain control over the laws under which they must live.

Historically, this safety valve was intended to rein in an out-of-control, massively powerful Congress that was attempting to destroy the rights of citizens. In the current age, however, Congress has lost control of substantive legislative matters to the administrative agencies and the courts. It has also lost control of spending, through its failure to regularly appropriate monies to operate the government in the manner it authorizes. Losing control of our laws to the unelected administrative state is just as serious a matter as having a power-hungry Congress. In both instances, citizens suffer the loss of their rights, in the first instance by an abusive Congress and in the second instance by unelected kakistocrats, who determine what our laws mean, how they are enforced, and what punishments are applied in the name of the kakistocracy.

In such a situation, state legislatures represent the only possibility for citizens to gain control over a system in which Congress has lost the ability to legislate and to check the powers of the other branches of government.

As the states have never successfully called for a convention for the purpose of proposing amendments to the Constitution, there are many unanswered procedural questions on an endless list that will be raised to block any movement by state legislatures to initiate a Convention of States. But the process of initiating a state application procedure for a Constitutional Convention is straightforward. While the process requires two-thirds of the states to call for a convention and three-fourths to ratify an amendment, the process can start when one state files an application with Congress, which acts purely as administrator. Congress has no authority to stop the process. While Congress must treat all states equally, its role is primarily to determine when two-thirds of the states have filed applications addressing a similar subject matter. Congress does, however, have the power to determine the method of ratification, either by the legislatures of three-fourths of the states or by conventions in three-fourth of the states. Other than that, Congress must call a convention for the purpose of proposing amendments to the Constitution when two-thirds of the states file similar applications.

Since 1789, state legislatures have submitted more than four hundred applications for a convention to consider a wide variety of issues, from a balanced budget amendment to abortion to prayer in public schools. None of the applications have ever reached the two-thirds threshold of thirty-four states. The balanced budget amendment did receive applications at one point from thirty-two state legislatures.

Though the state applications do not need to be identical, they must contain the same subject matter if Congress is to count them as similar for the purpose of calling a convention. Otherwise, Congress would reject the applications so as to avoid any effort to limit its power. Moreover, by using similar subject matter in the applications, the legislatures avoid charges of actions beyond the directions of the legislatures. The state legislatures must constantly be mindful of the fact that almost every kakistocrat and their collabortakers will be searching for flaws so as to void the process. With this in mind, state legislatures truly interested in playing their rightful constitutional role in our system of government should negotiate uniform language that can be adopted by the respective legislatures in advance of the first application.

Such language could be as simple as the following:

> An application to Congress for the purpose of calling a convention for the purpose of proposing amendments to the Constitution of the United States to determine the extent of Congress's power to regulate under the Commerce Clause, to define the scope of the General Welfare Clause in terms of public purpose, and to determine which is the most appropriate level of government for carrying out the many activities of government and the reallocation of those powers to the respective governments.

Part IV

Restructuring the Automatic Withdrawals of Taxpayer Assets

How Well We Treat Our People Will Determine How Long Our Constitutional Republic Lasts

For decades, the kakistocracy has allowed the costs of Social Security, Medicare, Medicaid, and prescription drugs to increase to the point that these programs are costing more than $1.6 trillion per year and are projected to be insolvent in two decades. Social Security provides benefits to fifty-eight million retired citizens as well as widows and minor children of deceased workers. Medicare provides health insurance for fifty-one million citizens, and Medicaid provides some health insurance and other health coverage for sixty-two million low-income and disabled people.

The real concern for the kakistocracy is that these automatic withdrawals are now given to half of all American households and represent more than fifty percent of all federal government outlays. It is estimated that unless these outlays are controlled, they could reach seventy-five percent of all federal government spending in a few decades.

These programs are viewed in many different ways, depending on the citizen's place in the system. Some recipients believe they are entitled to the benefits; others believe they have fully paid for the programs through their payroll taxes; and some believe they should not have to pay to support the retirement and health-care benefits given to others. One commentator views the use of his payroll taxes to provide benefits to people who are retired, disabled, and less fortunate as a form of theft, under which, he argues, his labor is commandeered by the government for the benefit of others. Most critics of these programs, however, complain that costs must be reduced to control the growing federal debt, which is in excess of $21 trillion.

To view Social Security, Medicare, and Medicaid as only about the money means that it's about the money when the collabortakers don't want to spend it to benefit the Dutiful Cogs, but when spending massive amounts of taxpayer money is important to the collabortakers, it is deemed essential for job creation and remaining competitive.

Over the last several decades, there has been a rapid increase in wealth inequality, with the well-off being the primary beneficiaries, receiving, some estimate, an additional $1.2 trillion in annual wealth, while the working class has been stuck in economic neutral. For instance, in 1980 the disparity in pay between a CEO and an average employee was forty-two to one. By 2014 it was three hundred and fifty-four to one.

The magnitude of income inequality can result from many factors other than just hard work: the family one is born into, inheritance, connections, better education, continuous good health care, government influence, or better nutrition. The collabortakers are just better off than the average working person. They are able to increase and transfer more of their wealth to their offspring and friends, who start at a higher rung on the ladder than the people who work at essential jobs to keep society running, such as picking up our garbage; cleaning our bathrooms; servicing our cars; or serving in the military to protect our country, our property, and our lives.

Few citizens want to take from the collabortakers just to take their money. That is not what Americans do! The concern of the average worker is to provide food and shelter for his or her family, have health care when sick, and retire with some dignity. The tension arises between the kakistocrats and collabortakers and the Dutiful Cogs when, in the name of reducing the nation's massive debt, the kakistocrats and collabortakers seek to reduce the Dutiful Cog's ability to get government benefits for food, shelter, and basic health care.

When this tension arises, the collabortakers usually frame the debate in terms of the high costs to provide benefits to the middle and lower classes. And while the collabortakers are correct that Social

Security, Medicare and Medicaid, and prescription drugs are wreaking havoc on our budget and debt burden, they conveniently forget that in the great recession of 2008, the federal government, using taxpayer money and debt borrowed from future generations, provided hundreds of billions of dollars to a banking system that created and sold financial instruments that were worthless, thus causing its collapse. A similar bailout occurred in the 1980s savings and loan crisis.

When the beachfront homes of the wealthy are flooded in hurricanes, it is subsidies provided by the federal government for insurance for the collabortakers that rebuild them. When corporate pension plans are raided, it is the federal government that insures the losses caused by the CEOs. Or the hedge fund manager pays a lower tax rate than the secretary because of legal maneuvering in the tax code. Or those who receive employer-sponsored health care have the benefit of it being tax-free, and the employer gets to deduct the benefit as a cost of doing business. Just that benefit alone is a $144 billion subsidy to corporations and certain employees. Workers who are not provided with employer-based health insurance pay the full cost. Then there is the mortgage interest deduction, another $77 billion annual benefit to the collabortakers.

Simply, trillions of taxpayer dollars provide subsidies to the collabortakers. Why are these subsidies not so massively unaffordable? The simple answer is that they are important to the collabortakers.

Complicating the elected kakistocrats' ability to quickly reduce or repeal these "entitlements" is the fact that they promised to protect these benefits from cuts in return for the citizens keeping them in public office. Such promises have gone on for decades, and as such, the kakistocrats should be legally estopped from substantially reducing them, since the giving of benefits was a scheme perpetrated by the kakistocracy and collabortakers to induce the American people to alter their tendency of providing for themselves and, instead, rely upon the promises of the kakistocracy to provide benefits.

Some elected kakistocrats will assert they can change the laws at will, including the laws that provide Social Security, Medicare and Medicaid, and prescription drug benefits. They will assert that there is nothing to bar their actions, as the doctrine of sovereign immunity bars citizens from suing the government. The kakistocrats may be legally correct under current legal principles. It is for this reason that the nation must immediately face up to the reality that it cannot afford the benefits given to its citizens, and that all the risk of the promises made by the kakistocracy falls on us. And when the kakistocracy defaults on its promises, there will be no one for us to punish, as those who made the promises will be long gone from public office and living well on pensions provided by us. It is up to us to act!

The American people not only need to hear the truth; they need to hear solutions, so they can make decisions on whom to elect.

In 2002, Professor Peter R. Fisher commented that "the federal government is an insurance company with an army." As more than 50 percent of the $4 trillion federal budget goes to programs that are viewed as social insurance (approximately $1.6 trillion) or to interest on the debt (approximately $433 billion) from the kakistocracy borrowing money to pay for the insurance programs, the federal government is truly an insurance company with an army.

The question before the American people is not when to restructure Social Security, Medicare, Medicaid, and prescription drug benefits. Rather, the question is how we can immediately restructure these programs to ensure a long-term acceptable and sustainable distribution of resources. Included in this restructuring must be the debt imposed on future generations. We cannot be so selfish as to take for our enjoyment today and place all the debt on our children. If we are not willing to pay for the present and future benefits we receive, then the nation will cease to exist, and all of us will be on the ash heap of history.

As we consider our options to pay for our benefits, we need to recognize that the elected kakistocrats do not have the courage to be honest with us. But we need to be honest with them. The citizens of this nation need to be presented with realistic alternatives for solving these issues, and we need to vigorously debate them so that the kakistocrats understand where we stand and do not need to stretch their limited courage.

The Kakistocracy Can Easily
Fix Social Security

After almost eighty years of solvency, the Social Security program is now running at a deficit, with a $39 billion deficit in 2014, which will dramatically increase due to the aging of the population. It is estimated that Social Security will be insolvent by 2035, yet in the next seventy-five years, more than seventy-seven million Americans will retire, and most will depend on it for at least some of their livelihood.

The good news is that Social Security can easily be made solvent through straightforward changes to the program, all of which will require some sacrifice. Sacrifice is not what anyone wants to hear, let alone pay for, but by addressing the issue now we may be able to avoid insolvency of the Social Security program in 2035.

The kakistocrats must level with the American people, because in the end, we as a nation can no longer allow ourselves to believe the illusion that we will continue to receive Social Security benefits without some changes to the program. The changes need to occur now. The American people will not only understand straightforward talk, they will appreciate it.

It is very likely that the American people will accept changes to Social Security to make the program solvent for the next seventy-five years if they believe the government is being honest with them and that they are not making the sacrifices so that the kakistocracy can flourish. To foster this discussion, the elected kakistocrats must hold a voluntary referendum that lays out the options for making Social Security solvent for the next seventy-five years, including the cost of each option. Once these options are on the table and the public discusses them, a consensus will begin to form around saving the program or a willingness to accept reduced benefits. Without this discussion and referendum, the public will continue to believe that they will receive benefits under the current system—until the flood-waters of reality drown their illusions in debt.

A few options for the referendum are as follows:

1. Raise the cap on income subject to Social Security taxes. The 2017 cap on taxable income is $127,200. In 1977, Congress adjusted the maximum taxable earnings to increase with wage growth. Over time, the maximum tax-able earnings subject to Social Security tax has increased from $16,500 in 1977 to the current $127,200. In 1977, Congress intended the cap to cover 90 percent of taxable wages. Today, however, wages under the cap only cover around 80 percent of taxable wages. To return to Congress's original statutory intent, the cap would have to be set at $270,000. Only about eight percent of the workforce would be impacted by this increase. As taxes on income to pay for Social Security are the most regressive, this increase would add equality to the system by making a few more high-income earners pay a little more of their income for Social Security to be saved.

2. Eliminate the cap entirely by having all taxable income subject to Social Security tax. While this would subject rich and poor to the same tax rate, it would subject the wealthiest in society to a significant tax increase. Under this scenario, however, both the Dutiful Cog and the wealthy would pay the tax to the full extent of their income.

3. Increase the amount of payroll taxes we pay. The Social Security trustees state that by raising payroll taxes paid by 2.83 percent (1.42 percent each for employer and employee), the program would be solvent through 2091. This would be a significant tax increase on those with lower incomes.

4. Subject all income to Social Security tax. Under this sce-nario, all fringe benefits paid to workers would be subject

to Social Security tax. This would again bring equality to the taxes imposed on workers. Presently, benefits like health insurance are not subject to Social Security tax. This means that those who receive employer-paid health insurance are not taxed on the fringe benefit compensation, while those without employer-paid benefits must pay the Social Security tax on income used to purchase health insurance. According to the economist Martin Feldstein, employers pay more than $1 trillion a year to provide health insurance to sixty percent of American workers. By subjecting these benefits to taxation, Social Security would receive an additional $135 billion annually, and by 2030 the trust fund would be in balance and continue to increase in solvency.

5. Since we are all living longer, the age to receive full Social Security benefits should be raised from the current sixty-seven for individuals born after 1960 to seventy for individuals born after 1965, and for individuals born 1970 or later, full retirement should start at age seventy-two. By partially conforming retirement age with increased life expectancy, the Social Security Trust Fund would be increased by hundreds of billions of dollars over the next few decades.

6. Do some combination of the above, so that every American has a stake in the decision, that is, gradually raise both the income cap and the retirement age, increase the payroll tax by some percentage, and tax some percentage of fringe benefits.

7. Do nothing and let the Social Security System go insolvent. Insolvency would start around 2035 with the reduction of benefits. If this path is taken, Congress and the Social Security trustees will have to reduce benefits to the amount that can be collected from taxes, and chaos will ensue.

Other realistic options should be added to the list. Once the list is final, Congress should circulate the options as widely as possible and inform the American people that it will ask them to discuss the options and vote in a referendum. The American people should be given at least six months to discuss the options. During that time, every member of Congress should talk to their constituents about the options, the consequences, and the importance of voting.

Having the referendum will engage the American people, as they will feel that they have a stake in the policies set by the kakistocracy. The results of the referendum will at least inform Congress as to what the American people are willing to pay to keep Social Security solvent. If they are not willing to pay for solvency, Congress will need to adjust Social Security benefits to make the program last as long as it can. At this point, Congress is honest with its citizens, and the decades of misleading them that Social Security benefits will never be reduced will be in the past.

Fixing Health Care Will Require the Wisdom of Our Founders

Unlike Social Security, there are no easy solutions to address the fact that sick people must be provided with health care, yet the rising cost of treatment is unsustainable in our economy. Moreover, as the cost of health care is now eighteen percent of the entire economy, there needs to be a policy that balances the needs of the people with the resources of the nation that can be spent on health care. Trying to achieve such a balance will be difficult because our medical system is currently designed to allow those who control it to determine who benefits from the massive amounts of money it is given.

The cost of health care has been rising faster than the rate of inflation for decades, and the kakistocracy has been unable to control the increasing costs. This should not be a surprise, as the health-care system is designed by the medical profession and insurance companies to be completely opaque. It does not disclose the cost of any service, it does not disclose agreements between providers and insurance companies as to reimbursement levels, and the medical and prescription drug industries are the only industries that are guaranteed a basic payment for their services. Complicating the situation, the United States gives high-level patent protection to the drug industry to ensure that it makes a return on its investment in research, yet the drug industry gouges us by charging several times more for its products than it charges the rest of the world.

In short, our medical system is controlled by a medical-insurance-drug complex ("MIDcomplex"), which is a merger of state and corporate power, namely, the kakistocracy and the collabortakers.

This MIDcomplex operates to amass wealth for its members at the expense of the nation's health.

This MIDcomplex of third-party insurance reimbursements to medical providers replaced the historical practice of doctors billing patients for services. This new system became common after World War II, when the nation was under wage controls and corporations started providing health benefit packages to attract workers. The third-party reimbursement package expanded over time, to the point where employers now provide medical insurance coverage for sixty percent of the workforce, while the government pays almost sixty percent of the nation's total medical bill, as employer-paid benefits are nontaxable to workers or employers. While this is a significant benefit, the downside is that those who are not as fortunate must find other ways to pay for medical services—purchase more expensive insurance as an individual or pay out of pocket, neither of which is tax-deductible. Many of the millions of people in this "on-your-own" group are small businesses, individuals, part-time workers, and the working poor who earn too much to receive government subsidies, but not enough to purchase health-care coverage. For the truly poor, disabled, and elderly, there is Medicaid or Medicare.

On top of these concerns, doctors prescribe medications that cost Americans two to sixteen times more than they cost in other countries. Doctors have the highest average income in the United States, and drug manufacturers have two to three times greater profits than our nation's largest automobile, oil and gas, and media companies.

It is estimated that our medical system costs us $3.0 trillion to $3.7 trillion annually, depending on what is considered a cost. It is the most expensive in the world. It is estimated that we pay $9,267 per person for medical care annually. Canada pays $4,351 per person, Germany $4,819 per person, and Japan $3,713 per person. The Organization for Economic Co-Operation and Development (OECD), an international organization that promotes policies that foster economic and social progress for the people of the world, ranks the costs of health care and life expectancy of its member countries. Excluding the United States, the average OECD country spends $3,226 per person annually on health care. In this study, the United States ranks fiftieth out of two hundred and twenty-one nations in the world in terms of life expectancy, and twenty-seventh out of the thirty-four industrialized countries. Clearly, we are not getting value for our money!

Providing service to patients is no longer the primary mission of the MIDcomplex. Rather, patients are merely commodities used in a process that produces massive profits. For decades, the kakistocracy has tinkered with fixing the system, and it has only gotten more expensive, which is not a surprise, as there is no competition, no transparency, and no outside oversight of the MIDcomplex. Are we so far down the path that we as a nation can no longer turn back? The better question is whether we as a nation can allow the kakistocracy and the MIDcomplex to continue taking us on the path to economic ruin?

If the MIDcomplex cannot be fixed by marginal changes, it must be completely restructured to ensure that medical treatment for patients is the focus, along with reasonable compensation for those involved in treating patients. Reasonable compensation would replace the excessive compensation now taken by the MIDcomplex under an opaque system, a majority of which is financed by the federal government through direct payments and indirect subsidies to, hospitals, doctors, insurance companies, employers, employees, the elderly, disabled and the poor. If the Dutiful Cogs of the nation are mandated to pay taxes for this inefficient system, their government must secure a more reasonable cost for the services provided.

The public literature on health-care reform focuses on some changes that should be considered to bring down cost and promote efficiency in the provision of services. Before Congress restructures the MIDcomplex, Congress should hold an exhaustive set of hearings to fully understand the MIDcomplex and alternatives for addressing the excessive costs in the system. Congress should start by examining many of the suggestions in the health literature for reducing costs and increasing quality. Some immediate suggestions from the literature that are worthy of consideration include the following:

1. Twenty-five to thirty percent of all monies spent to maintain the MIDcomplex is spent on administrative functions, such as billing. In a $3–$3.7 trillion industry, this would be

around \$750–\$900 billion annually. Surely there is some paperwork that can be reduced or eliminated.

2. Studies show that as much as thirty-three percent of the care provided is not associated with improved health. Surely this needs to be resolved and changes made to the system to achieve more effective outcomes.

3. Medicare is currently banned from negotiating prices with drug companies; therefore, patients pay the highest prices for the drugs prescribed. The elected kakistocrats must authorize Medicare to negotiate prices with drug companies.

4. The drug industry spends more money on marketing drugs, including opioids, than it does on research. The elected kakistocrats should reverse this trend by reducing subsidies for companies spending more on marketing than on research.

5. The billing of medical services must be made transparent by posting the cost of all services online.

6. For decades, the medical certification boards stood as a barrier to the establishment of new medical schools. Again, the MIDcomplex was allowed to build barriers to competition for the purpose of enhancing the personal compensation and profit for those within it. More medical schools must be built to address the projected shortage of forty-six thousand to ninety thousand doctors by 2025 due to retirement.

7. Greater authority should be given to nurse practitioners, so that the medical profession has more capacity to treat more people at a more reasonable cost.

8. Many more walk-in clinics should be established to deliver cheaper health care closer to where people live.

9. The nation should encourage foreign doctors to practice in the United States by offering them a path to citizenship if they serve patients in low-income, rural, and minority communities for a period of five years.

10. Doctors claim the high cost of malpractice insurance is a reason for ordering more tests and for early retirement. Limits should immediately be placed on damage awards, so

that the cost of malpractice insurance and the number of unnecessary and defensive tests can be reduced.

11. Corporations, trade associations, nonprofits, and labor unions should be authorized to form alliances to negotiate with the MIDcomplex for better prices and services.

12. Congress must immediately authorize the importation of drugs from countries that have safety standards equivalent to those set by our Food and Drug Administration.

13. The MIDcomplex must require its joint commission, which certifies hospital quality, to immediately inform the public of the hospitals that provide substandard, negligent, or harmful care.

14. The MIDcomplex must substantially reduce fraud or inappropriate care in the system, which is estimated to be $200 billion annually. One alternative is to impose treble damages on anyone convicted of fraudulent medical billing and prohibit the discharge of such fines in bankruptcy. This harsh punishment would create a serious disincentive to commit fraud.

15. The MIDcomplex should adopt the many new technologies that allow people to monitor their own health and to expand the use of telemedicine to reduce hospital visits, the costliest form of treatment.

Congress should continuously ask one question: what changes need to be made to bring health-care spending down to $6,950 per person, annually, which is about a twenty-five percent reduction in health-care costs. While this reduction may seem impossible, if made, the United States would still be spending more money per person than any other country in the world other than Switzerland.

The following are some modest proposals for consideration:

Modest Proposal 1: Let the MIDcomplex Restructure the Industry

As the federal government pays approximately sixty percent of the nation's health-care bill through direct payments, subsidies, and the tax deductions of employer-provided health insurance, and employers and individuals pay the rest, we Dutiful Cogs must demand that for these payments and subsidies to continue, the cost of health care must be reduced, and the quality of health care must be enhanced. Unfortunately, there is literally no law that can be passed that the MIDcomplex cannot find ways to circumvent. Therefore, it is suggested that the elected kakistocrats provide the MIDcomplex two years to produce a system that provides high-quality health care at a cost of $6,950 per person or less. The MIDcomplex knows how to balance costs with high-quality care. It just needs to decide whether it will undertake the challenge to maintain control of the health-care system or risk the consequences of having imposed on it alternative ways to achieve health-care sustainability.

A study by Alexis Pozen and David Cutler that analyzed the differences in the cost of medical services between Canada and the United States provides guidance as to where cost savings can be achieved. Pozen and Cutler found that the United States is more expensive in three categories: thirty-nine percent more costly in administrative expenses, thirty-one percent in higher salaries, and fourteen percent in additional procedures. Sixteen percent of the additional costs cannot be allocated.

If the MIDcomplex makes a proposal that reduces costs to make the health-care system more economically sustainable, it should be introduced and debated by Congress. Since Congress will have also been studying the intricacies of the health-care system, it should be able, as fiduciaries of the country, to use its collective knowledge and commonsense to fashion legislation that balances cost containment with quality medical care. If the MIDcomplex and Congress fail to produce a sustainable health-care law, Congress needs to recognize it does not have the competence to address this issue and should relinquish control over it to the states.

Modest Proposal 2: Declare Victory and Negotiate Federalism

Relinquishing control over the health-care issue means Congress is conceding that States, being far more knowledgeable of the needs of their citizens, must take over management of large parts of the health-care system while coordinating with states on other parts such as Medicare. Inherent in this concession is a recognition that each state has unique health-care issues and each state will address its needs in a way that best serves the state.

There will be challenges to this approach. Since states do not have the ability to print money, they will likely need financial assistance at least during the transition. Federal health-care programs that work such as Medicare will have to be integrated into the state program or remain as a stand-alone federal program. Like other federal programs that are administered by states, the federal and state governments will need to negotiate costs and responsibilities not only between governments but also between governments and citizens. To resolve this issue, all stakeholders must be involved.

Simply, in the final analysis states will only be able to design a health-care system that its citizens are willing to pay for. Governing is not easy, but we all need to participate so we know what we can achieve and what we are willing to pay for it. Within this governing process, it is essential that the MIDcomplex understand it is presently selling a service that is needed by everyone but not currently affordable to society. Only through administrative efficiency, cost-containment, better use of technology, and innovation can we produce a sustainable health-care delivery system.

Modest Proposal 3: Establish a Health-Care Budget

If Modest Proposals one and two fail to produce a system that can deliver quality health care to all Americans at a sustainable cost, Congress is left with no choice but to establish a health-care budget that the nation can afford and provide whatever health-care services it can provide with the monies available. There is no other choice if we are to avoid risking economic destruction.

Finally, faced with the possibility of dealing with a health-care budget, which will be the most unattractive of the alternatives, it is likely that the MIDcomplex will find ways to use technology, innovation, and smart business practices to substantially lower the cost of delivering high-quality health care to the American people. Otherwise, the participants in the MIDcomplex will be forced to continuously fight among themselves for a smaller and smaller share of the health-care budget.

Taxes: Eliminate Complexity, Unfairness, and Tax-Avoidance Schemes

Taxes need to be paid to keep the government working solely for the benefit of the American people and provide only the services needed to promote the general welfare, not the welfare of specific entities, classes, or individuals. Taxes should not be used to reward or punish interest groups or segments of the citizenry. Taxes should be easy to pay, fair, neutral, and transparent in application, and Congress should not use them to drive the policy decisions of the nation.

Our current tax system is anything but fair, neutral, and transparent. With more than twenty-five thousand pages of unreadable text containing provisions related to every activity of life and benefits for any group that can afford a lobbyist, it is a corrupt document that allows the collabortakers to manipulate tax benefits for themselves at the expense of the many. It is a document that allows Congress to reward friends, punish enemies, and demean Dutiful Cogs.

Every attempt at tax reform is nothing more than tinkering around the margins of the tax laws to provide more benefits to those who already reap the benefits of society. The wealthy continuously assert that they pay the bulk of individual income taxes, with the top ten percent of income earners paying seventy percent and the top one percent of the wealthy paying forty percent of all individual income taxes.

These distributional federal income tax statistics tell a technically correct story. The other story, however, is that the federal income tax code very effectively transfers the wealth of the nation to the wealthiest of the collabortakers. Over the last three decades, the

149

federal income tax laws, the corporate compensation structure, and the many laws that benefit and shift income have dramatically altered the recipients of the nation's wealth. Thirty years ago, the income disparity between the American CEO's and the average employee was forty-two to one. Today, it is three hundred and fifty-four to one. During the same time period, wealth inequality spread dramatically, with the top one percent increasing their ownership of the nation's wealth from below thirty percent in 1980 to more than forty percent today. And the top one-tenth of one percent of the wealthiest increased their ownership of the nation's wealth from seven percent to twenty-two percent over the same period. Numerous studies indicate that since 1990, most of the wage growth has gone to the top one percent, and wage growth for the middle sixty percent of workers has been stagnant.

How did this occur? The collabortakers, who are highly wealthy top managers of corporations and connected lobbyists, placed their friends in key political positions and on their boards of directors. As part of a reciprocal relationship, they protected each other, thus ensuring greater wealth for all in their class. These collabortakers skillfully used the tax laws to set up pass-through entities like carried-interest structures and partnerships to reduce their income and lower their individual tax rates. These maneuvers, combined with generation-skipping trusts; the placement of personal property in trust to avoid taxes; deferred compensation; tax credits for favored entities; direct subsidies, like farm subsidies for insurance companies; tax-exempt massive fringe benefits in health insurance and life insurance; the tax-free use of limousines and private aircraft provided them by corporations; and almost unlimited expense accounts transferred massive amounts of wealth to the already wealthy with little tax liability.

In the new tax law signed into law in December 2017, the collabortakers attempted to eliminate the estate tax, a twenty-three percent tax imposed on estates valued at more than $5 million for an individual and $11 million for a couple. Fewer than six thousand out of nearly three million estates annually are subject to this tax. Only the wealthiest of the wealthy pay it, yet the wealthy want us to believe that it must be eliminated to protect all small businesses. The collabortakers were, however, successful in convincing the kakistocracy to double the estate tax exemption to $11.2 million per decedent while still allowing a stepped-up basis so that future generations have fewer assets subject to estate tax.

This estate tax is essential for three reasons. First is the law of compound interest. This point may seem out of place, but Albert Einstein called the law of compound interest the greatest mathematical discovery of all time. Compound interest is a function of generating earnings on the reinvestment of money. There are only two components to it: the amount of the investment and the length of time the money is allowed to accumulate. The more money one invests, and the longer the investment generates income, the more money is generated. Because today many of the collabortakers are the one-percenters, the longer their assets continue to grow without being taxed, the more of the nation's wealth they accumulate. Without a tax upon the owner's death, these massive assets are freely transferred to future generations of the same family. Without the tax, these future generations, without any merit on their part, will continue to accumulate greater amounts of wealth, and therefore more and more of the nation's wealth is concentrated in fewer families. According to economist Edward N. Wolff the wealthiest one percent of households own more than the bottom ninety percent of households combined. If this is left unchecked, there will not even be cake for the masses or concern for the nation.

The second point is just as simple: the wealthiest can manipulate the tax code so that labor is taxed at a substantially higher rate than capital. This, coupled with a monetary policy that essentially provides interest-free money to the wealthy through Federal Reserve policy and federal government bailouts to financial institutions for losses due to excessive risk-taking to generate profits, ensures that the wealthiest among us have all the gains while the Dutiful Cogs assume all the losses.

The third component that allows collabortakers to multiply their wealth without being taxed is the use of the stepped-up basis on all inherited assets, thereby avoiding any taxes on the realized profits when the asset is sold. This, combined with Einstein's law of compound interest, ensures that the wealth of collabortakers multiplies without taxation, while the wealth of Dutiful Cogs remains flat and immediately taxed.

While collabortakers avoid paying taxes on income and accumulated wealth for years or many lifetimes within a family, Dutiful Cogs pay more and more regressive taxes. A regressive tax is defined as a tax imposed in such a manner that the tax rate decreases as the amount subject to taxation increases. These regressive taxes consume a significant part of Dutiful Cogs' income, yet they are insignificant to wealthy collabortakers because the income that can be taxed is small compared to the overall income. Taxes for Social Security, sales, gasoline and excise taxes, and license fees are extremely regressive and paid by Dutiful Cogs to keep the nation operating.

The collabortakers focus on the federal income tax and claim they pay too much of the cost of running the nation, yet millions of Dutiful Cogs pay taxes at every level of human activity while working in the mills to produce products many of them can't buy, or in-service establishments that keep the collabortakers comfortable, or in the army to protect the wealth of the collabortakers. How can collabortakers claim they need lower taxes when they are accumulating more of the nation's wealth while the Dutiful Cogs merely run in place or fall behind as they age?

The end story is that federal income tax is only one of the burdens borne by citizens. We are a nation that has always worked for a better tomorrow for ourselves, our children, and posterity. When we as a nation look at taxation, we need to look at it comprehensively.

The United States has never been a nation that supports class warfare, but the wealthiest need to appreciate the wisdom of Henry Ford, who sparked his own industrial revolution by paying his workers enough to be able to purchase the products they made. To continue this quest, the nation must develop a federal tax code that is simple, fair, and transparent and that only taxes us for what the federal government must do to protect us and our liberties. Every citizen must be able to read and understand the tax code in under an hour. We must create a new tax system that is not twenty-five thousand pages long, drafted by collabortakers, and designed by them to avoid paying taxes. The nation needs a tax code that allows an average citizen to understand what the government is charging for its services.

A modest proposal to achieve this goal would include the following:

Eliminate the Federal Corporate Income Tax

Corporations are merely organizations to generate wealth by providing society with needed products and services and pass the wealth to their owners, managers, employees, suppliers, consultants, or others who provide services. They are merely pass-through organizations, and as such, taxes should be imposed on those who are paid for the labor, goods, and services provided or contracted for. At times, individuals will function like a corporation, and when in that capacity, they should be treated like a corporation.

By eliminating the federal corporate income tax, the United States immediately becomes the most tax-competitive nation in the world. If the claims of the corporations are correct—that the taxes are a real burden on their competitiveness—eliminating corporate taxes should attract businesses from all over the world, so we can make products for the world and create massive numbers of new jobs in America. With all the new jobs, there will be new wealth, more income for the Dutiful Cogs, and, yes, more tax revenue for the nation.

Make All Gross Income Taxable: No Deductions, Exemptions, Credits, Nothing!

While this might seem like an impossible idea, it merely follows Amendment XVI of the US Constitution, which reads:

> The Congress shall have power to lay and collect taxes on incomes, from whatever source derived, without apportionment among the several States, and without regard to any census or enumeration.

Moreover, "gross income" as defined in the current Internal Revenue Code at title 26, section 61, includes:

> ...all income from whatever source derived including (but not limited to) the following items:
>
> (1) Compensation for services, including fees, commissions, fringe benefits, and similar items
> (2) Gross income derived from business
> (3) Gains derived from dealings in property
> (4) Interest
> (5) Rents
> (6) Royalties
> (7) Dividends
> (8) Alimony and separate maintenance payments
> (9) Annuities
> (10) Income from life insurance and endowment contracts
> (11) Pensions
> (12) Income from discharge of indebtedness
> (13) Distributive share of partnership gross income
> (14) Income in respect of a decedent
> (15) Income from an interest in an estate or trust

By taxing all gross income, every American would be subject to the same fair, simple, and transparent income tax, at every tax rate. By taxing all sources of income, the tax rate could be substantially lowered, since the base of taxed sources would be substantially larger. With all sources of income taxed, the collabortakers will be unable to manipulate the tax code to their benefit, something they have done since the first amendments to the federal income tax code were enacted by Congress in 1918.

TAXES: ELIMINATE COMPLEXITY, UNFAIRNESS, AND TAX-AVOIDANCE SCHEMES

Here are a few examples of new sources of income that, if taxed, would allow the federal government to substantially reduce the tax rates imposed on individuals while creating a simplified, more equitable tax system that substantially eliminates mechanisms that allow individuals to game the tax system, thus requiring others to make up the difference for funding the government. These changes would include the following:

- Eliminate the home mortgage deduction, which provides $77 billion dollars in deductions to certain homeowners who can itemize.
- Eliminate the deduction for employer-paid health insurance, which is a $144 billion tax-savings to those individuals lucky enough to have employer-paid health insurance.
- Tax hedge-fund managers at the same rate as the working person; this would make tens of billions subject to taxation.
- Tax heirs on the value of the asset at time of original purchase rather than allowing them to value the asset at the time of transfer. This change would make hundreds of billions of dollars of income subject to taxation. It would also start to control the law of compound interest that allows the wealthiest the ability to accumulate and transfer funds tax free at a much greater rate than the rest of society.
- Treat the benefits given to corporate CEOs, such as box seats at sporting and cultural events, as income, thus making billions of dollars of available income subject to taxation.
- Treat all fringe benefits as exactly what they are—compensation (income) to attract and retain employees, thereby subjecting all employees to the same tax for the same income.
- Eliminate the hundreds, if not thousands, of special interest provisions in the current tax code, thereby making billions of dollars in income subject to taxation.
- Subject to some reasonable gift-tax exemption, tax the remaining amount of wealth transfers, either gifts or estate

transfers, as income, thus establishing a system that has the broadest tax base possible so that it can tax at lower rates.

Utilizing the original 1913 tax structure would make the payment of taxes simple, fair, and transparent for both the individual and government. Income taxed would be at the lowest rate possible because the base for tax collecting would be as broad as possible. Individuals would determine their income from all sources, subtract any deductions (the amount of income not subject to tax, e.g., $30,000 to provide an incentive for everyone to work), and multiply the remaining amount by the percent of tax due on income, for example: five percent on amounts more than $30,000 and not exceeding $50,000, seven percent on amounts more than $50,000 and not exceeding $75,000, nine percent on amounts more than $75,000 but not exceeding $100,000, and additional ranges up to a rate cap of twenty-two percent.

Under this structure, citizens would easily understand the amount of income going to the government to perform services for them. Simply, this type of a structure would be real truth in the cost of government. Moreover, eliminating all the deductions, except for the $30,000 work incentive, would place all taxpayers on an equal footing and would significantly reduce the ability of individuals to manipulate the tax-paying system.

To prevent tax fraud within this simple process, the penalties, like the penalties in the original 1913 tax law, would need to be stiff, perhaps double the amount of tax not paid plus criminal prosecution for fraud and intentional evasion of taxes. Such high penalties place all individuals on notice that those who do not pay their share of taxes in amounts legally owed would be punished. This is essential, as those who do not pay their fair share of taxes merely transfer the cost to honest citizens in the form of additional taxes. This so-called tax gap (income hidden from the government) is estimated to cost the Treasury more than $450 billion annually. Just based on the new sources of income listed above, along with collecting tax gap revenue, new tax revenues would generate enough new income for the

Treasury to drop the highest marginal tax rate to its lowest in history for individuals.

This absurd proposal is more than doable; it is, in fact, similar to the first income tax code in 1913. The entire 1913 Internal Revenue Service Form 1040 was four pages long, including instructions. On the 1913 Form 1040, people or corporations listed their income and commonsense deductions for necessary business expenses and losses, interest on debt, taxes paid to state and local governments to avoid double taxation, and depreciation of assets used in the business. The deductions were subtracted from income and the tax was applied. That was it! The primary difference between what is being proposed and the 1913 IRS Form 1040, is there would be no corporate income tax and even the few individual deductions on the 1913 Form 1040, e.g. state taxes, would be eliminated.

Unfortunately, beginning with the first amendments to the tax code in 1918, the collabortakers took it from a four-page form that could be completed with little effort to twenty-five thousand pages of laws and regulations, making it their tool of choice for transferring benefits to themselves.

Part V

Citizen Management
of the Kakistocracy

It Is Now!

There are times in the history of a nation when the people of the nation, its real owners, need to act before those entrusted with the control and resources of the nation cause it great harm. If there was ever a time in the history of this republic when the people of the nation need to regain control over those governing the nation, it is now! If there was ever a time in the history of human events that we the people have the means, ability, and opportunity to exercise control over our government, it is now!

Our present government has little understanding of or concern for the well-being of the nation or the plight of its people. The kakistocracy's concern is maintaining power over us and our resources. As owners of the nation, we all must realize that we have a personal stake in its continued greatness. As owners, it is our responsibility to ensure that the country is run in a manner that best serves and protects the present and posterity as an indivisible unit. We are one nation, and we truly do stand or fall together as an indivisible unit. Unfortunately, the kakistocracy has forgotten this fact.

The history of government is a continuous struggle between those who govern and those who live under its dictates. This nation's belief is that we can form a government of limited powers that promotes maximum freedom and security of the individual in an organized society. Within this framework, those who control the structure of the government have no rights other than what the Constitution and people give them. While this point is routinely forgotten, except in lip service to citizens (usually around election time), it is time for all citizens to recognize the simple fact that the kakistocrats who control our government have become separated from us. We citizens are viewed as subjects of a government that does not remember that its powers come from us.

We the people have let down our country by not demanding that those entrusted with running it act as responsible servants and fiduciaries to the people and trustees of our assets, knowledgeable of our issues and competent in the management of the daily affairs of the nation that they voluntarily sought to assume.

Today, we citizens have the tools to constitutionally regain control over those who occupy the structure of government that we elect, pay for, and live under. We must fix a government that is broken. For as long as we remain prisoners of a broken government, we cannot compete in a world in which wealth and jobs can move out of this country at the speed of light while leaving us with massive government debt, promises that cannot be honored, families and communities without jobs, and a government that seeks to have its citizens be followers but not participants. The time is now for the real owners of the country, its citizens, to develop mechanisms to ensure that the government is limited and financially sound, protects liberty and the security of the nation, and, above all, operates according to the Constitution.

Principles for Citizen Management of the Kakistocracy

As citizens, we must recognize that we will never be able to control the actions of the kakistocrats, simply because those seeking positions in the kakistocracy and their collabortakers seek only one thing: power over us, our actions, and our wealth. And because the human mind is usually able to maneuver around any restrictions imposed on it, the kakistocrats will always be able to evade any constitution or law to secure their wants. Therefore, our concern as Americans should not be to control the kakistocrats and their collabortakers but to create a government structure that allows us to manage their actions.

Originally, the US Constitution was the structure to manage the actions of the kakistocrats, but the kakistocrats, being who they are, continuously work to turn limited constitutional government into almost unlimited government; to delegate congressional responsibilities, such as only Congress can declare war, into prerogatives of the executive; and to twist the promotion of the general welfare into the promotion of welfare for kakistocrats and collabortakers.

The judiciary has also had a major role in cementing the powers of the kakistocracy. At the very beginning of our republic, the judiciary superimposed the English common-law doctrine of sovereign immunity onto the American Constitution, a doctrine that says, "the king can do no wrong." By imposing this doctrine, the judiciary created a structure in which those governing us became a separate power by prohibiting suits against the government. From that point forward, sovereign immunity became the super constitutional provision that limited citizens' ability to hold their government accountable. Sovereign immunity is mentioned nowhere in the Constitution. It has been imposed on us and our Constitution by the courts for the sole reason of making the government more powerful than the people. Simply, today sovereign immunity is the doctrine that the kakistocracy can do no wrong.

Taking on the kakistocracy will be no easy task, but it can be done. It can be done by monitoring it and having a solid foundation in facts to challenge it when it exceeds its authority. Although we are limited in making the kakistocracy legally accountable while in office, we can make it fearful of losing status and power by the following:

1. Constantly reminding the kakistocrats that they work for us, and the benefits they give themselves and their collabor-takers are the wealth of the nation.

2. Making the kakistocrats personally liable when they transgress the Constitution. Such liability will make them more cautious, less arrogant, and more respectful of the laws they impose on us.

3. Requiring that every law and regulation imposed on us apply equally to the kakistocracy.

4. Promoting transparency of responsibility by listing on the internet the names and responsibilities of all members of the kakistocracy. We pay them; we need to know who they are and what they are doing for us and to us.

5. Voiding the doctrine of sovereign immunity, because in the final analysis, the main problem is not the kakistocrats—it is our inability to hold them responsible for their actions.

6. Imposing de facto term limits on every congressional kakistocrat by voting against any who have more than twelve years of elected service.

7. Demanding that all kakistocrats in Congress:
    a. Impose term limits on kakistocrats in the bureaucracy;
    b. Pledge to serve as a check on the other branches of government, rather than serving merely as a check on another political party;

c.   Pledge that they will not fund any war unless declared by Congress;

d.   Pledge to operate Congress in regular order so the people of this nation can determine the appropriateness of their decisions;

e.   Refuse to fund programs not authorized by Congress;

f.   Disclose all monies spent by the kakistocracy, other than for national security reasons, at the time payment is made, including all information regarding the recipient of the funds and the purpose for payment;

g.   Require all monies expended by any individual or organization to influence the kakistocracy be publicly disclosed at the time payment is made, including all payments and contributions by third parties to organizations that are established to influence the kakistocracy;

h.   Mandate that all decisions of the kakistocracy that rely on studies, reports, or data be accompanied by the release of all supporting data, so the public can determine the validity of the data used for decision-making;

i.   Require all federal elected officials, employees, and government contractors to publish their daily work calendars; and

j.   Limit compensation, including benefits and pensions, paid to federal employees to no more than what is paid for similar positions in the private sector.

Citizens Must Demand That Elected Kakistocrats Take the Gift Clause Pledge

Because the kakistocrats on their own will never voluntarily agree to stop giving away our money to their friends and political supporters, all of us Dutiful Cogs must demand of every person running for political office to take the gift clause pledge.

> I pledge that, as a member of Congress, I will not vote to give, grant, or loan public funds or to extend the credit of the public to any private corporation, association, or private undertaking, and neither shall I vote to allow public funds to be used for the purpose of taking stock or investing in private corporations or any other private undertaking.

A similar pledge must be asked of all candidates running for president. That pledge would be:

> I pledge that, as president of the United States, I will not sign any law or allow any member of my administration to give, grant, or loan public funds or to extend the credit of the public to any private corporation, association, or private undertaking, and neither shall I allow public funds to be used for the purpose of taking stock

or investing in private corporations or any other
private undertaking.

By asking each person seeking election to the US Congress
and running for president to take the pledge, the taxpayers will easily know which kakistocrats are more inclined to protect the public monies we send to the government. If the pledge is broken, the
public will know who is trustworthy and who is not. Breach of the
pledge is self-evident to the citizens, accountability is easily mea-
sured, and recourse is defeat in the next election for the kakistocrat
and his or her party.

Establish a Citizen Information Center

Perhaps the most serious legislative and regulatory deficiency in the kakistocracy is a lack of sound scientific, economic, and statistical information. Congress operates almost exclusively on what is provided to it by lobbyists, witnesses, and collabortakers, with little ability to determine the soundness of the information.

While executive branch agencies hire contractors to perform many studies, the studies produced mostly support the position the agency wants to establish. The final agency decisions can be reviewed by the courts. It is rare, however, that a court would review the validity of the science, economics, or statistics; rather, all the court determines is whether the agency acted rationally in relying on such materials. And because the agency paid to have the studies developed to support its determination, its decision generally looks rational to the reviewing court, without reviewing the soundness of the studies.

Without sound, tested information, our lawmakers make policies to achieve political outcomes rather than sound policy outcomes. In Washington, DC, it is often stated that "politics trumps policy all the time." This outcome must be reversed if this nation is to produce sound policy.

The kakistocrats want to make political decisions, not sound policy decisions; therefore, it is up to us to create a mechanism that produces unbiased, sound, peer-reviewed information that is available to the kakistocracy for policy making. If sound information is developed, it will be difficult for the kakistocracy to ignore it. Moreover, producing such information will diminish the value of the information produced by lobbyists, political operatives, and collabortakers.

A citizen information center would be simple to create and easy to finance. It would be established for the sole purpose of developing information needed for policy development, such as regarding health care, immigration, or taxes. It would carry out unbiased, original research in major policy areas so that the facts of the issue are sound. Every major study would be subject to peer review, and all studies, along with all underlying information and the peer-reviewed report, would be made public. Imagine having the health-care debate knowing how money flows in the system, who receives it, what procedures actually cost, and the development of facts as to why our health-care system costs more than that of any other country in the world. It would be a considerably different debate, one centered on facts, not the one-page fact sheets or advertisements of interest groups.

Funding this much-needed undertaking would be cheap if only half the Dutiful Cogs participated. There are more than two hundred and twenty-eight million adults in the United States. If half the adults made a ten-dollar donation to the center annually, approximately $1.4 billion would be raised to fund its research, an amount sufficient to run a large, highly talented, nonpolitical fact-development organization. The sound, peer-reviewed output of the center would be hard for the kakistocracy and the collabortakers to ignore. Moreover, when the collabortakers supply conflicting data to the kakistocracy, they would have to explain why their data is better. Once the debate over data begins, the public wins, as the costs and benefits of the decision must be clearly discussed in light of the facts. In the final analysis, good-quality data produces sound policy.

Once this sound, peer-viewed data is in the public domain, anyone could use it to support or challenge the decisions made by the kakistocracy and the data used by collabortakers and special interest groups.

Citizens Can Start a Glorious Constitutional Revolution

While some citizens may call for the state legislatures to apply for an Article V convention to make amendments to the US Constitution, such an effort could take years or decades, likely without any meaningful results. There are more efficient ways to return this nation to a constitutional republic. Our Constitution gives us the power to start a revolution every other year. We can do it peacefully and legally, notwithstanding the fact that we would be overthrowing the kakistocracy. It is called voting, and voting is truly a revolutionary mechanism. Voting in a constitutional republic is the quickest and most effective revolutionary tool that could ever be given to citizens to change their government.

To start the revolution, we citizens need to recruit four hundred and thirty-five individuals who possess lots of common sense to run in every House of Representatives congressional district in the nation as independent candidates for Congress. We would also need to recruit thirty-three individuals to run as independents for each Senate seat up for a vote in that year. Citizens in every congressional district in the nation should hold local conventions to select citizens who will challenge the kakistocracy by promising to restore Congress to the primary legislative body of the nation and for its members to act as fiduciaries of our interests, limit the size of government, devolve powers to the states, take the gift clause pledge, and limit themselves to twelve years of total service.

After selecting these independent candidates for Congress, the Dutiful Cogs must help them gather the signatures they need to secure a place on the ballot and campaign. This would not be as difficult a task as it might appear. These local conventions would receive national attention as they would be the first nationwide effort by ordinary citizens to reclaim their government from the kakistocracy. The issues being discussed would give new hope to large segments of our citizenry, who are now cynical about a system that ignores them and that they do not believe can be changed.

Money would not be the lifeblood of these local congressional contests. Look at the Cantor race in Virginia in 2014, when the majority leader of the House of Representatives was defeated by an unknown challenger with little money to fund the campaign. But the voters made up for the lack of money. In these circumstances, dedication to principle overrides all concerns. No one would be expected to raise large sums of money for campaigns. Advertising the campaigns of these independents across the country would be done by the movement itself. It would be the people's constitutional revolution. It would be a simple affirmation that the citizens are taking the nation back from the kakistocracy. Once the word gets out about this constitutional revolution, people throughout the nation will lend their support to the cause with their votes. Citizens of the nation will fully understand the significance of the movement and that its result will free them from the tyranny of the kakistocracy that is every bit as autocratic as King George.

A groundswell of support will occur for all these regular citizens running for Congress, these Dutiful Cogs, asking for a chance to run the country for a limited period of time. Imagine people who work every day of their lives, who deal with the details of living, running the nation. These are people who know about paying bills and appreciate the difficulty of working and managing a family, all coming together to keep our nation functioning by applying common sense to issues created by people. Again, imagine all that common sense in one place, in Congress. These will be people who know that if you only have a dollar, you can only spend a dollar—and maybe not all of it, as you must save for rainy days.

Calling for these local congressional nominating conventions would provide us with a specific opportunity to take the system back in a short period of time and to begin making it work for us, on constitutional terms. Obviously, there are many issues confronting this nation, and they will not be addressed in one term of Congress. But we need to stop walking down the path of decline and start the process of rebuilding the nation with citizens who will serve as fiduciaries.

If anyone doubts that such a constitutional revolution can be started and won in a two-year time span, look no further than the anti-establishment victory of Donald Trump, who took an escalator down to cheering supporters and took on sixteen opponents and a Democratic nominee who was ordained to be the next president of the country. Then there is Emmanuel Macron in France: having never held elected office, he formed his own political party and won the presidency at thirty-nine years of age.

Then there is Sebastian Kurz, a thirty-one-year-old, whose People's Party ran for the first time in the Austrian election and who secured enough votes to become chancellor of Austria and gain the right to form a coalition government. Also, there is Andrej Babis, a multibillionaire who formed the Action for Dissatisfied Citizens Party in the Czech Republic and won sufficient votes to form a new coalition government. Finally, there is the new president of Mexico, Andres Manuel Lopez Obrardor, a national populist who was twice defeated for his very anti-establishment views. He soundly defeated Mexico's Institutional Revolutionary Party which had controlled the government for eighty years.

Whether one agrees with the policies of Trump, Macron, Kurz, Babis, or Lopez Obrardor, the point is clear—constitutional revolutions can happen, they have recently happened, and it is now up to the Dutiful Cogs to complete the next stage of the constitutional revolution.

States Can Start a Glorious Constitutional Revolution

There are a few actions the states can immediately initiate before undertaking the arduous, time-consuming process of having two-thirds of the state legislatures call for a convention to propose amendments to the Constitution. First and foremost, the states must appreciate that in the system of cooperative federalism they like the federal government are sovereigns. And yes, while there is federal supremacy on issues of federal law, the federal government cannot be commander, with the states its servants. It is for this reason that the federal government makes grants to states to incentivize them to implement hundreds of federal programs. Simply, the federal government needs voluntary cooperation by the states if it is to have any ability to implement its mandates. Without such incentives and cooperation, a massive number of federal mandates would be ignored, because the federal government would not have the resources to implement the programs in the states.

Moreover, it is rare that federal contributions cover the full costs of state implementation. For example, under environmental law, the states implement more than ninety percent of federally delegated programs but receive only thirty percent of the cost of implementation. Without state resources supplementing federal mandates, federal programs could not be implemented by the federal government. The fact that Congress can't, or won't, pay states the full cost of program implementation gives the states great leverage over federal mandates.

To focus the attention of the federal government on its out-of-control mandates, the states need to stop implementing a few programs this year and a few next year. Eventually, these state refusals to implement federal programs will place enough stress on the kakistocracy to force it to align priorities with resources. This will substantially rein in out-of-control federal overreach.

It should be noted that a state's refusal to implement a federal program is not in any manner nullification, which is deeming a federal law unconstitutional. On the contrary, states may recognize federal law but refuse to implement it. In such instances, the federal government must implement its own laws, which requires far more resources than the kakistocracy has. Therefore, if the kakistocracy is to continue with its out-of-control mandates, the simple answer is to let it find the resources to implement the overreach.

Another pressure point of state leverage against the federal government is the many deadlines in federal law mandating that states implement or rewrite regulations within strict time frames. For example, federal environmental laws require states to implement numerous updates of Clean Air Act regulations in short periods of time, such as every five years. Such short time frames turn federal mandates into a never-ending process that imposes new requirements before the existing requirements are implemented. Complicating this is the fact that the federal agencies miss many of the deadlines under which they must act. This places even more pressure on states to act in an even shorter period of time.

To address this federal regulatory game of piling more and more demands on states, the states, under federal administrative law, could sue the federal government every time it misses a statutory deadline, which occurs hundreds of times a year. These lawsuits would earn the states not only a seat in the courtroom but also a seat that allows the litigating states to negotiate with the kakistocracy over the development of a reasonable regulatory structure that can be implemented with available resources. If the law is to be the law, then the kakistocracy must also be mandated to obey it. The kakistocracy cannot force states to obey its orders while ignoring its responsibilities to comply with statutorily imposed deadlines on it.

In the final analysis, aggressive state action would demonstrate to the kakistocracy the unreasonableness of the overwhelming number of federal mandates. These state actions would open up discussions with the federal government on which level of government should implement and pay for a specific government program. If these actions fail to tame the kakistocracy, then the states must undertake the arduous, time-consuming process of organizing two-thirds of the state legislatures to apply for a Constitutional Convention. If such action is necessary, both the legislatures of the respective states and their citizens will know the kakistocracy can no longer function as a federal government and must be changed by constitutional amendment.

What Would Devolution of Federal Government Powers to the States Look Like?

If, as proposed, the United States devolves much of its domestic policy (e.g., housing, energy, environment) to the states, the kakistocracy would have thousands of fewer details to administer every day, thus freeing it up to focus on the primary functions of a national government: defense of the nation, strength of the currency, reduction of massive deficits, soundness of the banking system, immigration and securing the borders, and concrete actions to ensure the free flow of interstate and foreign commerce.

Getting these problems under control will place the United States on a solid foundation to lead the world for another century. If we do not get these problems under control, we will eventually be consumed by financial and internal chaos and rapidly declining military strength. Simply, some nation that we owe money to will want to be repaid, and the United States will not be able to pay or will repay with worthless dollars. What happens—default? War? Or do we become a reckless nuclear power like others in the world today?

Also, when the kakistocracy devolves power to the states, that would strengthen our system of federalism; with less power and money in Washington, not only will the kakistocracy shrink, but it will want to shrink, as it will have less and less access to the wealth of the nation. Moreover, devolving many programs to the states would truly create real-world competition between the competing political philosophy of limited government that stresses personal freedom and enterprise and those who believe that big government can best provide for the needs of the citizens.

Some citizens would cluster in places where the overall mind-set is citizen management of a limited government; an emphasis on hard work and being rewarded for it; wealth and job creation; and a fundamental belief that through the exercise of liberty today, tomorrow will always be better for citizens. Other citizens will seek out places where the overall mind-set is to promote a large government with many programs addressing the needs of its people and a willingness by those citizens to pay for the services being demanded. We should be all up for the challenge to determine which political philosophy will prevail and where.

The key change that will occur when power is devolved to the states will be the absence of the continuously running federal money-printing press. As the federal government begins to put its fiscal house in order, the states will have to address how to pay for the programs they create. The cost of big government will be borne by the people who want it. For a while, the high-spending states might borrow to pay bills, but without a federal money-printing press to bail out bankrupt states, the creditworthiness of high-spending states will be limited by the realities of the market.

In this situation, each state will have to compete for doctors, lawyers, artists, businesses, manufacturing, pilots, engineers, and every other occupation in society. Some citizens will go to increase their wealth, others will go for lifestyle, and others will go to states where the people are willing to provide greater government assistance than other states. The key is to find a state where people can live as they would like or be able to move to a state that fits how they want to live. This is not possible today, as the nation has been federalized by the kakistocracy; most, if not all, states administer the same federal programs, which the federal government keeps printing money to pay for.

The common denominator in devolution is that each state will have an opportunity to develop its distinct personality and economy. We all need to welcome the challenge to live as we believe, because devolution allows the nation to conduct a grand experiment that allows the application of different political philosophies while protecting the nation from bankruptcy by shrinking the expenditures of the federal government.

Going Forward

We Have Reached a Fork in the Road

Nations, like people, travel on many paths during their lives. With each path taken, character is formed, new traits are exhibited, creativity occurs, wisdom is obtained, yet wrongs are committed, callousness is acquired, apathy grows, and we become careless in our approach to governing ourselves. Yet we travel on. Though we cannot change any of the paths taken, we can determine the next path we take in light of where we are and where we want to go.

Today we must decide if we want to continue traveling the path the kakistocracy has set us on—or take the proverbial less traveled path that hopefully takes us to greater liberty, control of our property, and more opportunities within the framework of a smaller government, with powers dispersed among the federal government, the states, and our communities. The two paths truly do diverge, and the path we choose will make all the difference for the future of our country.

The path chosen by the kakistocracy is well known and well worn. It is the path of massive debt, a rapidly widening divide between the very wealthy and the Dutiful Cogs, uncontrolled spending, gifts to political friends, regulatory overreach and incompetence, laws to help friends, laws to punish enemies, and so many laws that the legal system is not comprehensible even to those who write and control it. The kakistocracy has passed so many laws that it can declare any person to be a criminal.

We are now a nation that is economically and philosophically exhausted from shouldering the growing weight of government. To paraphrase Winston Churchill, a curtain of debt, complexity, and political personal gain has descended across our nation. It is locking us into stagnation and mediocrity and dulling our spirit to imagine a bright future. And we are paying dearly for this dreadful state of being. We are now giving more than $4 trillion of our money every year to the kakistocracy to run our government, and such amounts are never enough, and we get few, if any, new or creative ideas for what we spend. All we hear are words of obfuscation from a kakistocracy that operates to separate us from our freedom.

In the introduction, there is a list of failed policies and programs inflicted upon us by the kakistocracy. The list is too long to repeat, but it is worth reading again. The failings of the kakistocracy are legion; the subsidies to collabortakers are massive, wasteful, and shameful; and the lack of any meaningful management of our government for the general welfare is appalling. The path the kakistocracy has placed us on is a path to ruin. Just like humans, nations do die, and we are no exception. At some point, that will happen to United States—that is a certainty—but it does not need to be now. We Dutiful Cogs have the power to take back management of the nation. The question, however, is, do we dare?

What will follow the kakistocracy is unknown, but as long as the transition to a smaller government is a working partnership between citizens and their federal and state governments, it will be accomplished through proper constitutional procedure. The transition will again prove that the nation is capable of exceptional acts that further liberty, protect property, and provide a framework in which we can all pursue happiness.

Congress must immediately wrest its constitutional power to legislate from the executive that runs the bureaucracy and devolve many powers to the states, so that our federal and state governments can function cooperatively and focus on priorities.

Congress can very easily lead the constitutional revolution by recognizing its fiduciary duty to us. Congress has the power to work with the states to simplify laws and government and distribute power to the most efficient level of government. A first step that Congress could take would be to live under the laws it imposes on us. No more exceptions, exemptions, or automatic raises. As part of the process, Congress must work in a normal order by allowing only the laws that it authorizes and reauthorizes to be implemented. Congress must cease deeming laws reauthorized when it has not performed the requisite oversight to understand whether the law is working as intended, and, if not, make the changes needed before reauthorizing and funding it for another period of time. This act alone will ensure that Congress understands and oversees the laws it passes and that our monies are appropriated only for what Congress finds worthy of continuing as laws we all must obey. This process will begin the long effort of simplifying and reducing our complex and massive body of law. And fewer laws mean fewer regulations; eventually the process will right itself, and we will be freer.

As we move forward by making our government more understandable and driving the implementation of law to its most efficient level, new laws will be more focused on achieving a purpose that truly serves the general welfare, not the welfare of kakistocrats and collabortakers.

In the final analysis, by lessening and redistributing the powers of the kakistocracy, the kakistocrats and their collabortakers will have less interest in government, because government will be a source of less wealth and less power. As government control lessens and simplicity of law and enforcement returns, American citizens will again see opportunities to create wealth and jobs for themselves. As the oppression of government excesses fade in citizens' memory, excitement will return in the form of innovation and appreciation that work is rewarded. When this connection is made, the people of this nation will again be on the path to being exceptional.

Finally, we must recognize that if our Congress is unwilling to serve as fiduciary and act as our legislative body, exercising powers that check the abuses of the executive and the courts, then we must exercise our absolute right to start a constitutional revolution that votes out every member of Congress and elects a real citizen legislature of committed, term-limited fiduciaries who truly act for the nation.

Today, at this moment, we are standing at a fork in the road. We can continue to follow the path the kakistocracy has set us on, or we can remake the nation in our image by choosing the path that returns us to the principles of smaller government divided among the states and the federal government and individual freedom. Whichever path we take, we and our posterity will reap the fruits of success or suffer the slide from being exceptional to experiencing the perpetual frustrations of mediocrity, growing poverty, and a dimmer future. The future is ours to create. We are at a fork in the road, and it is time for us Dutiful Cogs, not the kakistocracy, to choose the path we will travel on.

About the Author

William L. Kovacs has been involved in the nation's policy making process for four decades. He held positions as senior vice president for environment, technology & regulatory affairs for one of the largest and most influential trade associations in the county, chief counsel on Capitol Hill providing legislative counsel on two landmark laws in one Congress, chairman of a state environmental board and a partner in several Washington, DC law firms. He has testified before Congress thirty-nine times, participated in several hundred federal rule-makings, written policy and law review articles, and has given major policy presentations in forty-nine states. Now, in *Reform the Kakistocracy*, he describes the changes needed in federal policy to ensure a sustainable government and one manageable by citizens. Concurrent with the book, Kovacs writes regularly on government reform on his blog <u>reformthekakis-tocracy.com</u>.

CPSIA information can be obtained
at www.ICGtesting.com
Printed in the USA
BVHW031143221219
567501BV00001B/63/P